KEN EVANS

With photographs by
Nigel Higginson

The Kingswood Press

Typeset by Alacrity Phototypesetters,
Banwell Castle, Weston-super-Mare
Printed and bound in Great Britain by
Garden City Press, Letchworth

0 434 98066 8

Contents

Never be afraid to talk to a top rider or ask
for an autograph.

Introduction

This is the story of a BMX team and a BMX family, the two so closely interwoven that it's often difficult to see where one ends and the other begins. It is the story of the Ammaco team, the first big team in the history of British BMX, and still the number one squad; and of the Jarvis family, who first brought BMX bikes into Britain, who built the first BMX tracks, and who launched the sport in the UK. It is no wonder that they formed and still run the top squad in British Bicycle Moto-Cross.

What is it like to be a member of the Ammaco team? You only have to look at the crowds around the team van at any meeting, to know that every BMX rider would like to find out, first-hand.

It is the ambition of every rider to be sponsored. To get a "full factory" sponsorship is a dream come true. To go full-factory for Ammaco Mongoose is surely the ultimate.

Some riders have been with the team for several years. Others have joined Ammaco and moved on, like Tim March, Andy Ruffell, Cav Strutt, Nikki Matthews, Steve Gratton, Craig Schofield and Damien Myles, because no team could retain so many stars and remain a balanced unit.

Every season, to join their established stars, Ammaco recruits promising riders who seem to get a boost from donning the distinctive red, white and blue race gear. Yet it is not the gear, not even the bikes, which brings out the best in the Ammaco recruits. It is the unique atmosphere of the team, virtually a family in its own right.

Through this book you can sample the atmosphere of the Ammaco team, meet its riders and manager. You will learn how BMX started up in Britain, and get a taste of the big-time action which is BMX today.

And while you are reading, you can learn to improve your BMX riding and racing through the advice of the Ammaco riders. After all, they are the ones who you will have to meet — and one day even beat.

One of the world's best riders — and he's
British. Tim March.

Try to keep your bike straight as it lands.
Here Garry Llewellyn is having a job to follow
this rule.

Once the team van is unpacked, the first job is to put the bikes together. (*Evans*)

Just Another Weekend

Travel with the Ammaco team on a typical racing trip

It's early Saturday morning at the Jarvis house deep in Kent, and Sue Jarvis is trying to make the switch from being mother of five children to being team manager of 12 BMX riders. It isn't really much of a change, because five of the riders are her children, and the rest need a lot of mothering anyway.

In fact, the weekend started even earlier. Ever since Thursday, Sue has been chivvying her "dirty dozen" to make sure they are ready for the weekend's event. Last weekend was a muddy one, and it's taken days to clean out the van, get the mud off the bikes, and generally repair the physical and mechanical damage done. The Jarvis kids have a checklist to go through, to make sure everything is prepared for departure. In the meantime, as Saturday was getting nearer and nearer, Sue had to get on the phone to other team members, checking that they had solved their particular problems, or whether they needed any new gear for the weekend to come.

Breakfast is hardly cleared away, and the big Transit van is half-packed. Even though the team vehicle is well fitted out, it is still a squeeze to fit in eight riders and their long-suffering manager, plus the bags and the bikes, the spares, the first-aid box, the Ammaco Mon-goose publicity brochures — and of course an enormous amount of food. It is up to each rider to make sure that their personal bag and bike are on board — that way if anything is left behind, the rider has only himself or herself to blame.

While Alexia, Holly, Sam, Russell and Julian Jarvis are getting their gear together, Garry and Wayne Llewellyn and red-haired Pete Middleton turn up. The party is now complete; Jon Greaves and father Ken (an Ammaco area sales manager) will be coming with Dylan Clayton under their own steam from Southport, Keely Mulkerrins from Twickenham, and David Morris from Trowbridge.

There's a long way to go. The Ammaco Mongoose team has to ride at all the 11 National meetings of UKBMX — one of two governing bodies of BMX — and other top events too. So travelling is the rule rather than the exception. They spend most Saturday nights at a hotel, and sometimes Friday nights too, if the race is very far away.

In the team van the conversation ranges from the latest crankset to the latest cassette, or anything else to keep the boredom at bay. In the end, everyone looks forward to stopping for a meal — which is usually chips with anything.

Finally, the van turns into the entrance of the track. It's early afternoon and there are only a handful of other vehicles already parked there. Tomorrow there will be hundreds, and even later today there will be a lot more, many of them with tents pitched outside.

Although the event takes only a Sunday, it is virtually impossible to arrive on the day itself and still give of your best. The riders need to recover from the journey, of course, but most of all they need to get used to the track.

The van parked, the doors open and the motley crew that is the travel-weary Ammaco squad piles out. Some members, short of sleep and cramped, are a trifle irritable. Tempers are a bit on edge until contact with the track starts to help them unwind.

The bikes, complete except for the removed front wheels, are parked on the nearest patch of ground, ready for final assembly and checking. "Whose is this disgusting item?" asks Sue Jarvis of one machine still unmistakably bearing the dust from last weekend's venue. She knows the answer already, of course, since each bike bears an individual look. Small son Sam is fixed with a withering glare. Glowering down from six feet four in the stratosphere, Garry Llewellyn is also disapproving. His bike, readily identifiable by the lilac power disc, is spotless.

Holly Jarvis needs a little help, and Pete Middleton, at the opposite end of the team age scale, steps in to provide it. Her bike is as important as his.

Rivals and friends from other teams drift over to chat and swap impressions about the track or the latest BMX gossip. But for the Ammaco crew, now is not the time to chat. Tomorrow's race starts here and now, with practice.

First chore is scrutineering. Every race bike has to be checked before it is allowed on the track, whether its owner is a pro or a novice. Holly is first to the scrutineering enclosure, eager to get practising. A big race official checks her bike for unnecessary sharp edges, loose parts, or anything that might fail and cause a crash.

Not surprisingly, the bike passes the test, as does Holly's race clothing — crash helmet, gloves, long trousers and sleeves must be worn. The "reward" is a coloured sticker for the race

number plate, which allows the bike and its rider on to the track. The weekend's event is expected to attract so many riders that not all can practice at once, so the colour of the sticker also indicates which practice sessions she is allowed.

One of the other factory team riders drifts up to the team van and gives his verdict on the track. "It's long and it's boring".

A typical track takes about 30 seconds to race around. This one will need about 50 seconds for the best men to cover it. For the younger riders this is bad news, since it means the bigger ones in their age group will have a strength advantage, and clever riding won't count as much.

There are big problems for one of the other team members, who has cross-threaded a pedal putting it into the crank. Normally the bikes are loaded into the van with pedals removed, because they are more easily packed that way. Pedal and crank threads are both damaged, so have to be changed.

"Go and find someone who's selling," says Sue, whose stock of spare parts doesn't run to a crank. At every big BMX meeting there are vans from BMX shops who set up stalls and do a roaring trade, some from badly-needed spare parts, but mostly because all BMX enthusiasts like to have something new and bang-up-to-date.

On this occasion a crank is borrowed from another team. Although BMX brings big rivalries on the track, it seems to make just as big friendships off it.

With all the bikes and riders ready to practise or already practising, manager Sue's job is done for a while. She knows that all the team have officially registered for tomorrow's racing, but there are more than a thousand others to be signed on.

The team always arrive early because of her official commitment to the sport. She is national secretary of UKBMX, the governing body, an unpaid post which involves many hours of work every week. At meetings she pitches in to help the local race organization team with any job that needs doing, and at the same time ensures that the national regulations of UKBMX are followed.

Every rider has different ideas of how to

Alexia Jarvis will put
her own machine together as well.

The tightest line through the berm
isn't always the fastest, as Andy
Ruffell shows here.

Alexia Jarvis in the smart
race gear of an Ammaco factory
team rider.

practise and how long practice should take. If the track is new or unfamiliar, extra time is needed to get to know its starting-gate; berms, jumps and even the way its surface is best handled. The more dedicated riders walk the course, looking for every pothole or subtle change of surface quality. Finding the best and smoothest line around the track can sometimes make the difference between winning and losing.

On a familiar track, all that is really needed is enough practice starts and riding to make sure that nothing has been changed, to loosen off legs made stiff through hours of travelling, and to test the bike in race conditions.

Once practice is over, it's on to the hotel, for a rest, a rap session, and the restaurant. Ammaco's riders spend a lot of time resting on hotel beds, rapping with their mates, and waiting for the time when they can go down and try to eat the hotel out of business. This is no longer as expensive a process as it used to be, thanks to a low-price deal negotiated by UKBMX with a big hotel chain. It means that the hotel corridors are full of BMX riders in race gear and tee-shirts with a BMX flavour.

After dinner, Sue does the rounds to try to see that everyone gets a reasonably early night. Inevitably she is never completely successful, since Pete, Wayne and Garry are difficult to tear away from the hotel games room and its computer games.

On the morning of the race, alarm calls all round ensure that the team members are early down to breakfast. Even the biggest hotels find it quite a tough prospect serving thirteen mouths at once.

Back at the track, the picture is completely different from that of the previous day. The parking area is jammed with vehicles, and with the tents of riders who preferred to stay the night under canvas. There are long queues for scrutineering and registration. The Ammaco van is directed into a special area reserved for factory teams, and of course they have no scrutineering worries because that job was done yesterday.

Sue inspects the team members once more, making sure that their race clothing is smart and a credit to the sponsors, even to a check of each number plate to make sure that the right co-sponsor stickers are present and correct.

With UKBMX duties pressing, she now has to leave the team to their own resources, and that works very well. After all, they know where the spare food is kept, and now need bother her only for the occasional cash hand-out when the stock of Mars bars runs low.

Moto sheets are posted, which means the Ammacos know in which races they are riding. Wayne, Garry, David and Julian all have two moto numbers to remember, because they also ride 24-inch wheeled cruiser motos.

The racing starts, and early competitor Holly has a racing set-back. There are a few tears. Comforting words from Pete and a hug from Mum do the trick, and in the second moto series she wins. The older riders, especially Pete and Wayne, watch out for the younger ones. A tactical mistake usually brings helpful advice.

In between motos, riders have different ways of easing or building the tension, depending on whether they like to race relaxed or wound-up like a coiled spring. Jon and Dylan tinker with their bikes. Wayne wanders around signing autographs. Garry is over near the start-hill, intently watching the starter and trying to predict when he will drop the gate. Alexia and Holly are less intense, swapping tales with friends.

There is a momentary gasp from the crowd during the pro moto, and there is Pete sprawling on the dirt. He tried to go through a gap that wasn't there, and paid the penalty. Sometimes he tries to go through a gap that isn't there and creates one. Although there is a first-aid kit in the van it isn't needed here. All race casualties have to be treated by St John's attendants — a UKBMX ruling. In this case it's a few more grazes to grace the Middleton legs. They say you can judge a top rider's determination by his scars.

The racing moves on through semi-finals to finals, and the eliminated members leave the van to shout for their team-mates who have made it through. They aren't the only ones shouting for the Ammaco colours, because the team's friendly attitude has brought much popularity.

It's trophy time, and the Ammacos have racked up five. Not a bad day for any team, but not a good one in comparison. The trophies get loaded in the van alongside the muddied Mongooses and their tired owners. Time to depart. On the way home an hour's sleep for the lucky ones, and a meal for them all. For most, it's school tomorrow, when they don another kind of uniform, while the Ammaco gear goes into the wash.

Just another weekend

BMX By Accident

How the bikes and the sport came to Britain – and the man who bought them

Lots of crazes which "make it big" in the United States of America never even reach Britain. For Ten years, BMX was one of the crazes which didn't happen over here. Then, in 1980, things started to change, and inside twelve months it became pretty clear that Bicycle Moto-Cross was here to stay.

It still might not have happened but for the vision and determination of one man, Ammaco's managing director Malcolm Jarvis, who had no background at all in pedal-cycles of any kind.

In 1979 he decided that his business — building high-quality houses — didn't have too bright a future, so he looked around for something else to do, and started to dabble in importing and exporting machinery. This developed into a small importing business handling 10-speed bikes, which in turn took him to visit the Milan Cycle Show in November that year.

The Milan exhibition, held every two years, is effectively the world cycle show, and all new developments appear here so that the cycle trade from many countries can see, comment and — the manufacturers hope — place orders. Nowadays every cycle manufacturer features a range of BMX bikes, and some make nothing other than BMX. Way back in 1979 BMX bikes in Europe were rare.

But you have to remember that Malcolm's background wasn't in cycling, so it didn't matter to him that the BMX bikes he spotted in Milan were so revolutionary they scared most buyers. His sporting background was in moto-cross, rally-cross and trials riding. And when he saw those bikes, he knew that there was big business to be done in Great Britain with them.

"What grabbed me straight away was the sheer efficiency of performance of the BMX bikes," Malcolm recalls now. "They were uncluttered, their structure was simple and just shouted out to be ridden fast. They looked as though they were made to be ridden anywhere — and fast."

When he got back from Milan he wasted no more time, and jumped on the first plane to Los Angeles, on the West Coast of the USA.

"All I knew was that BMX was over there somewhere. I didn't go to Los Angeles for any particular reason, other than the thought that I would start on the West and move Eastwards until I found it."

In fact he didn't have far to go. He booked into a hotel in Long Beach, a California beach resort, and picked up the telephone directory to see if BMX was listed in any form. He found the number of a magazine, BMX-Plus, and called them.

"They were very surprised to hear from me,

and I was quite pleased to find that they were only half a mile down the road from the hotel. I went down to see them, and that was the start of everything. I was there for about seven days, just gathering information and trying to get some bikes to sell."

In that period he visited SE Racing, owned by Scott Breithaupt, reckoned to be the founder of BMX. At Redline he met Stu Thompson, and the blonde BMX Superstar even let Malcolm road test his own bike. He was introduced to a young man who liked nothing better than to do stunts on his BMX bike, and for a living cut out chunks of plastic and turned them into race number-plates. That young man was Bob Haro, who was to become the greatest BMX Freestyle rider of his generation. And everywhere Malcolm made notes, took photos, and pointed his video camera.

"And I went to the Mongoose factory and met Skip Hess. Of the BMX outfits I saw, their factory was the biggest and the most professional. I decided that they were the bikes to go for."

The next problem was how to pass on his

Britain's first BMX track, in the back garden of the Jarvis family. *(Ammaco)*

own enthusiasm for BMX to the people he hoped would buy Mongoose bikes.

"How do you bring a sport over from the States to Britain? I decided the best way was through magazines. I bought back the first couple of hundred copies of the BMX mags after I had agreed to take 10,000 copies and distribute them. In the end I think we moved 18,000 in the first year."

During that American trip, the first of many, he saw several BMX meetings. "It struck me that the key to the appeal of BMX was that it was one single pass of the track, not lap after lap. The whole thing was over in seconds, but during that short time you could re-create the thrills of motor-cycle racing. And you could watch race after race in a short time."

He was convinced that the British would take up the sport enthusiastically. "After all, we were the nation that started trials and scrambling. Our very breeding made us naturals for a sport like this. We have much more of a daredevil spirit than some other countries."

Once back in Britain, armed with BMX bikes for the Jarvis children as well as for display, Malcolm and his company set about popularizing the sport in general, and Mongoose bikes in particular. They organized displays for cycle-shop owners all over the country, printed leaflets to introduce the sport and to give basic instruction on track design, and sent them to 3000 addresses.

But the reaction from cycle dealers was unenthusiastic. "It will never catch on," and "It will be another expensive craze like skate-boards" were typical comments. A better reaction came from the former skateboard and roller-skate shops, which were used to catering for the youngsters and alive to the trends.

"I was surprised at the initial bad reaction, but not discouraged by it," says Malcolm. "Because the kids loved it, and their reaction from day one was so enthusiastic, we had no negative thoughts. It was almost like magic, that wherever we took a BMX bike, so fifty kids would turn up from nowhere to see it."

Established British bike manufacturers were slow to catch on to the BMX boom that was to follow. It was two years before Raleigh, the Nottingham cycle manufacturing giant, produced a BMX bike. Other manufacturers still don't have BMX in their product range.

"After about six months, when a number of magazines had become excited about BMX and written about it, I felt there was sufficient power behind BMX to keep it rolling. By that time Halfords and Puch were behind it, and Halfords made a significant contribution. By Autumn of 1980 there was no stopping BMX in this country."

Initially the big problem had been the lack of BMX tracks. Although the bikes could be ridden on any patch of rough ground, this couldn't be the same as a real race track. Malcolm, himself a civil engineer, set about getting tracks built.

"The first one was in our own back garden. We raced there seven days a week. All the local kids would come around because there was nowhere else. They would all watch the videos I'd taken in California, and practise the freestyle stunts that Bob Haro had done in front of my camera."

Buckmore Park at Chatham, scene of the first organized meeting. Leading this event is Sam Jarvis. (*Ammaco*)

The next tracks built under the Mongoose banner were at Buckmore Park in Chatham, Albury in Hertfordshire, and even one in Scotland.

The first Mongoose team was formed with lads local to Tenterden in Kent, where the Jarvises live to this day. They were good riders, but purely locals. But as time went on, the team started signing up really promising riders. Andy Ruffell came late in 1980, Pete Middleton early the following year. Sam Jarvis, then only four, was doing well for the family.

From this you can see that Ammaco and the man behind it were doing a lot more than just selling bikes and raking in the profits. In fact, with the amount spent on getting the sport launched, one wonders if there were any profits in those early years.

"I don't think, even now, that we put too much into BMX. We recognized just how much

In October 1980 this winners' link-up includes (*from left*) Sam Jarvis, Russ Jarvis, Pete Middleton, Nikki Matthews, Cav Strutt and Andy Ruffell. (*Ammaco*)

we were doing, and realized that inevitably other BMX bike companies would benefit from our efforts. But I felt we had to do it because if we didn't, no one else could have done it so well or so quickly, because of the skills we had at our fingertips."

Malcolm's civil engineering background meant that track design and construction were comparatively easy for him. He even had construction plant available.

All the same, he and Sue were happy when they received a visit from two guys wanting to start UKBMX, a body to govern the sport nationally, and to continue promoting it. It meant that Malcolm could spend more time looking to

boost the Mongoose name as the market for BMX bikes mushroomed.

"I was glad to see it develop that way. In the UK it is much more of a family sport than in the USA. Over there the sport is controlled partly by commercial interests and organization. Here at least the organization is on an independent and amateur basis, for the people and by the people."

He never forgets that BMX racing is for the kids. One day at Buckmore Park always reminds him of that.

"I woke up on the day of the meeting and it was two feet deep in snow outside. We went down to Buckmore Park and it was four feet deep, so I cancelled the meeting. You couldn't even see the track. The kids were furious, because they still wanted to ride. After that I made the decision never to cancel another meet, whatever the weather."

Malcolm even raced a couple of times in those early days, and can still show the scar on his nose from a fall in the first National. At the beginning he went everywhere with the team, and he is still heavily involved. Although Mongoose bikes are imported from the States, the Ammaco bikes are made specially to Malcolm's own designs, based on experience from the team.

Practising what he preaches, Malcolm Jarvis leads this Ammaco staff event at a 1980 Buckmore Park meeting. (Ammaco)

"I talk to the riders about the equipment they use, get a feedback on the geometry of the bikes, how they handle. I make sure that they know Ammaco feels they are important.

"It's nice to have good results, but you don't have to be the best all the time. I just want a team which will present itself and the company to the public in a good way. And I rely on them to help me with design. Everything on the Ammaco bikes comes from what the riders tell me."

One question that people keep on asking about BMX is how long will it last. Malcolm's answer is quick and confident.

"It will last forever. A large proportion of kids have bikes, and they all like tracking on rough ground. The BMX bike is the best for the job because it's made that way. On top of that there is BMX racing, which offers so much colour, and has the potential to generate so much excitement at such a low cost. This excitement can spread to the whole family. BMX is anywhere, anytime. It just has to go on for ever."

Building the Whitaugh Park track in Scotland
was a family affair. *From left:* Holly, Alexia,
Julian, Sam, Russell and Sue. (*Ammaco*)

Keeping Them Going

Managing the Ammaco team is one of the sport's most demanding jobs. Sue Jarvis explains why – and recalls some of the highpoints of its history

What do you get if you cross a secretary, a teacher, a mum and a sheepdog? The answer is Ammaco's team manager, Sue Jarvis, who has and needs all these qualities to run the squad which, year after year, is voted top team by the fans.

She's no technical wizard, and would rather do most things than put a bike together.

"I keep out of the technical side and the tactics. The riders help each other out on those. I can't tell them how they should set their bikes up. My only concern is that the bikes should be clean and dripping with Ammaco transfers."

Away from weekends, her time is split being national secretary for UKBMX and running the Ammaco team from an office at her home in Tenterden. Oh, and she does have to run a household, not to mention five children.

It's probably the long experience of being mother to a quintet of kids that is her biggest qualification for team managership. Certainly her style of running the team is motherly rather than managerial. She reckons that works best.

"With other teams the manager/rider relationship is like between employer and employee. With us it's like a family, and of course there are a lot of my family in the team. I tend to bawl and shout a lot at them, and they sometimes bawl and shout back."

Until Tim March's wife took over the management of the March Racing team, Sue Jarvis was the only female BMX team manager. Did she find her sex an advantage or otherwise?

"It has to have been an advantage, because I was the only woman team manager and we ended up as the top team year after year."

She was never actually appointed manager..It just sort of happened. In the beginning both she and her husband Malcolm would naturally drive the local kids about and publicize Mongoose through their performances.

"I can remember that Anthony Woodcock was the cream of the crop then. He was a motocross rider, and really should have won everything," she recalls.

"At that time I organized the racing and provided the tuck box. Then one weekend Malcolm couldn't make it, and I had to do it all. It seemed to work, and since then Malcolm has been extremely reluctant to give me the sack."

It has worked out cheaper too, since manager and five of the team are based in the same place, which for a small company makes good financial sense.

Part of her job is to keep some kind of control on the finance, because even an average weekend will eat up £300 in expenses, and that's not counting the cost of materials. It would be even more but for the very special hotel rates she has managed to negotiate.

In an average year, the team will cost £50,000 to run. If a lot of foreign travel is involved, that sum will go up in leaps and pounds. The team van takes a pounding. Not only does it cover 10,000 miles every year just travelling to races, but it also has to suffer continual overloading, and the patter of not-so-tiny feet. They are now partway to exhausting team van number four.

She still supplies the tuck box. "I make acres and acres of food when we go away at weekends, which seems to last until about 10.30 on Saturday morning, and no one seems to have had anything. So then I have to keep on handing out money for Mars bars and burgers."

The team consumes not only food, but a seemingly endless supply of equipment. Every week, she finds someone needs something

Many big names have passed through the Ammaco team. This line-up includes Andy Ruffell (*far left*), Tim March (*third from left*) and Craig Schofield (*fourth from left*). With Pete Middleton (*far right*) they are all now top-flight riders. (*Ammaco*)

new, whether it's a pair of wheels or a pair of gloves. The cost mounts up.

"On average I reckon every rider needs two bikes every season, if you add all the bits and pieces together. On top of that, they each get through four sets of race gear — that's tee-shirts, tops, race pants, and anoraks for bad weather. On top of that they get gloves, one helmet and two pairs of shoes."

The bikes are pretty standard. At the start, they were all Mongoose bikes, but now they are mixed in with a few Ammaco models, which the team members have helped to design. If you keep a sharp eye out, you could see an Ammaco prototype of a new model to be launched in a future season. This is, after all, one of the uses of

Sometimes Sue Jarvis has to support her riders in deed as well as word. Garry Llewellyn (No. 14) in the finishing enclosure at a Kellogg's meeting gets the helping hand. *(Ammaco)*

a racing team.

"The team has a great influence on the styling of the bikes, not only the Ammacos, but also the Mongoose models. We don't build specials for our team the same way that some other factory teams do. The principle is that anyone should be able to go out and buy the kind of bike they've seen our guys winning on."

Running a BMX factory team is partly a sporting undertaking, but it has to have a commercial side too. The final result of having the team has to be good bike sales. So part of Sue's job is to ensure that the team works to boost Ammaco sales at the tracks, and any other places where BMX riders might gather.

"The team has a standard instruction that they have to be well-behaved and charming to people, to give the fans time, to sign autographs. And I think generally they follow this instruction, because each year we seem to get voted the top team by the fans."

The team is on call for all kinds of promotions, at shops, shows, galas, and to adver-

tising agencies which want a BMX flavour to their latest product.

Attracting co-sponsorship is another part of Sue's job. In return for using and promoting their product, she has attracted backing from Renthal (handlebars and seat posts), Boogie (number plates) and Sealink (ferry services). In addition, some riders have co-sponsorship deals individually with manufacturers of items which don't clash with Ammaco's lines. She has to make sure that every such deal is in the overall interests of the company as well as of the riders themselves.

And of course she has to keep the team itself in being. Although some members stay with Ammaco for years, others come and go. Tim March was once in Ammaco colours, and he left because he needed more publicity, and couldn't get it from a team where Andy Ruffell was the acknowledged top rider.

"We are the biggest factory team going. The strength is normally 12 or 13 on full-factory sponsorship, plus another 30 in our support team. They get help with equipment through their local dealer, which gives them some sponsorship and a chance to get into the factory team later."

She admits that these numbers are too high to keep husband Malcolm happy, but while the results are still good, it is difficult to cut down.

"The aim is to have riders in a variety of age groups, although not necessarily someone in every age group. Being a top team, we get approaches almost every day, everything from club-level riders to established stars, asking to join us. Apart from that, I'm watching the racing wherever we are, to see if there is anyone we might want for the future."

All those letters and phone calls asking for places in the team aren't disregarded. Any likely applications mean that Sue takes a special look at the rider concerned. She has to decide whether that rider, his level of performance and his temperament, will fit in with the existing squad. Sometimes the suggestions about possible new riders will come from current team members.

The next stage is a phone call or a meeting, a discussion with the rider and his or her parents. Finally, there is a letter of agreement drawn up, and Ammaco has a new team rider.

"It's not a contract, because the riders are too young to be held to contracts. So the agreement is nothing too strict. You have to remember that these are children you are dealing with, and you have to be fair and understanding to them. If a rider decides that he doesn't want to ride for you any more, then you shouldn't hold him to it, because even if you did, he wouldn't be riding his best for you."

Even so, team switching in mid-season is a problem. If a company goes to the expense of floating a team, it will usually have plenty of advertising material printed to support its effort — and it is costly to re-print if the team changes in the middle of the racing year. So

factory teams have worked out an agreement not to allow moves to new teams except in the winter.

Although it must be great for any rider to race BMX on a free bike, in free race gear, travelling all over the country with the sponsor picking up the tab, there has to be discipline. And one person provides it. The same person who makes it right with a hug and a comforting word when things go wrong.

"At times I'm a bit bossy," says Sue. "I have to be. It helps that I used to be a schoolteacher. That means I'm used to herding kids around, and accepting their changes in moods. And the team is just an extension of my family."

At the start there was criticism that the Mongoose squad had too many Jarvises in it. "That's all but disappeared now. Any of my children who have factory sponsorship get it because they deserve it." She points out that two of her sons do not get full team benefits.

Within the team, every member has equal status. Even though some riders are stars in the BMX magazines, they stay just another team member as far as Sue is concerned.

She knows that there will always be disciplinary problems, and recognizes the reason.

"All the best BMX-ers are basically rowdy kids. It is the aggressiveness and the uncaring streak that make them winners. I have the team with the winners but I also have the rowdiest team. You take some of the better-behaved kids and you'll find they won't be really great BMX riders."

Yes, she admits, there is bad behaviour in hotels sometimes, which leads to apologies and payments for damage caused. "When it happens I have the job of defending them first, and then later giving them a good telling-off. And of course there has to be a punishment." In one recent case the punishment was missing an international trip, which was a tough lesson.

Even though the team has been going only a few years, Sue already has a big store of memories, particularly of the riders who are household names today.

"Pete particularly had a rowdy reputation, but it wasn't all deserved. Certainly he would never walk away from trouble but he has a heart of gold, and he's a tremendous help to me in the team. I can tell that he will be one of the riders who will stay in BMX in some capacity to help the sport when he stops racing.

"And Wayne. When he first came to us he was a little fat thing who couldn't even stay on his bike. But what struck me was his determination to win. He would train and train, because he wanted to be the best."

Andy Ruffell, who was Ammaco's big draw-card for years until he moved to Raleigh for the 1985 season was, Sue recalls, "A scruffy little urchin. It amazed me how he would never let us down. He would arrive on time anywhere you told him, switch on the magic and draw a crowd. In 1980, our first year in BMX business, we went to the Cologne Cycle Show in Germany, and in the exhibition halls he borrowed a BMX bike from someone and started to do stunts in the aisle. The security guys, who are normally a bit serious, were just amazed to see what he could do. Then they realized he'd drawn such a crowd that no one could get by and they went into a flat panic to get it cleared."

Even her own youngest daughter Holly provides her shares of stories. "I remember how one day little Holly finished a race and then went over and told an official where he got off. She was giving him the verbals just like Pete would. I just wanted to crawl into a hole."

Then there was one notable incident when hotel bookings went wrong during the 1984 Kellogg's series, and Sue had to share a bedroom with Andy and Pete. "It didn't bother me, except that all the American riders kept popping by for a chat with the lads."

Overseas trips have been memorable too, and provided their share of tight spots. Like the day when the team was so late for the boat that they drove straight through passport control and customs at the French port. They caught the boat, but afterwards had an uncomfortable interview in the purser's cabin.

"Or the other occasion in France when Andy and Pete went for a wander in another French port, and when we found them they were just being picked up by the police and about to be carted off to jail. They'd wandered into a non-pedestrian zone and couldn't understand why

the police were shouting at them, and started to run."

It's not all trouble on overseas trips though. In 1983 the team enjoyed a fabulous three-week jaunt. "We first went to France for a demo, then on to Dijon for the second round of the Europeans, and finally to Slagharen in Holland for the world championships.

"For the first week we were down in the Ardeche, a lovely area of France, lots of mountains. We'd been invited down there to do demos because at that time the French sport was still getting going. The Ammacos were the best-known team in Europe, and they were greeted like heros. The lads loved all the attention they were getting from the local girls.

"It was a tremendous trip. There were 11 riders and me, plus bikes, luggage and camping gear just in case, all stuffed into a Volkswagen bus."

The "attention from girls" has increased as BMX has got more and more popular. "There is a groupie element almost everywhere we go," she says. "During the Kellogg's in 1985 there were three girls who hung around our hotel every day and all day, just waiting for Garry and Wayne."

There have been the inevitable crashes in the team's history, but nothing serious. "A couple of broken wrists, a broken thumb, Steve Greaves taken to hospital when he took a bang in his kidneys. But nothing lasting. To start with I got worried every time there was a fall. I'd look at the pile of bodies on the deck and swear they weren't going to get up. But of course, they almost always did. I've stopped worrying so much now.

"Which is not to say that I don't take an interest in the racing. I still jump up and down and shout when someone in the team is on the track, but I don't get upset if they don't win. I know that no one wants to win more than the riders themselves, so they will be more upset than me if they don't."

Line-up at the beginning of the 1985 season.
Back row, from left: Steve Greaves, Wayne
Llewellyn, Garry Llewellyn, Pete Middleton.
Middle row: Alexia Jarvis, Jon Greaves, Dylan
Clayton. Front row: Holly Jarvis, Sam Jarvis.
(*Ammaco*)

Dylan leads over a speed jump, using his arms to push the front wheel down.

Call for Dylan

The quiet one from Wigan, who just loves bikes

To Dylan Clayton, a fun evening could well be spent taking a BMX bike apart and putting it together again. For Dylan, a new signing for Ammaco 1985, loves to tinker with machinery.

If anyone on the team has a problem with a bearing or a brake, a crankset or a chain, they'll call for Dylan.

You might think that the quiet-spoken lad from Wigan is the team mechanic from this description, apart from one small detail. In 1984, in his first season of BMX, he took the number one plate in the 9-expert class. Now that's not easy.

"My brother bought me a BMX bike for Christmas, which was how I started. Once I'd started racing well I heard from a friend that the Robinson team were interested in signing me up, so at the next National my dad sort of walked past their van and Alan Woods, the sponsor, asked if he could speak to him about signing me."

Towards the end of the season Dylan already had his sights on a move to Ammaco: "At the Wigan National, on my local track, I asked Sam Jarvis to speak to his mum for me about joining the team. He did, and said I'd get my answer at the big indoor meeting in London at Olympia. As it happened, I won there, and Ammaco agreed to sign me for 1985."

The team quickly adopted him and nicknamed him "E.T.", although Dylan has yet to be spotted making his BMX bike fly for longer than a couple of seconds.

"At first I was shy, but now I'm friends with them all. I like the atmosphere in the team, because the older riders are always ready to help the younger ones. In 1984 I got the number one plate really because I was fast. I wasn't that good on tactics. Since I've joined Ammaco I've learned how to take berms and jumps better. If I make a mistake in a race, the others tell me what I did wrong, and how to do it better next time."

On the track, Dylan is "a bit of a daredevil — if I can't get out of the gate first, then I watch for the gaps. And if I see them, I go for them."

Despite this, he seldom crashes. "I hardly ever fall at Nationals. I probably crash more when I ride the midweek meetings at the Three Sisters track in Wigan. Even in my age group there's a fair amount of body contact in the racing. You have to come to terms with it. And, being number one, I find everyone is trying to put me under pressure. They know that I'm the one they have to beat."

Key to consistent high placings is, Dylan feels, the start. "My aim is to get out in front and stay there. For starts my technique is not to get

"Now where can I fit this chainring?" Dylan works out his next mechanical challenge.

(Evans)

up on the pedals until the starter says 'Riders ready!' Then, on 'Pedals ready!' I lean back, so that when the gate drops I snap my body forward to bring the weight down more on the pedals."

When you talk to Dylan you can see that he is a technician. Just in the same way he found out about bikes by taking his own apart and putting it back together again, time and time again, he has built up his own racing style and tactics by a lot of practice.

"I practise an awful lot, and usually race twice a week. I try to be on my bike as often as I can, although I don't take it on the streets."

Talk about his bike, and you find that he knows exactly how he likes it. "Crank length? I'm a spinner, so I prefer 170mm to 175, which I find much too long. Wheels are important. I run on Arayas with $1\frac{1}{8}$ tyres. I have thought of using sew-ups, but they're so difficult to repair. When I'm setting my position I like my handlebars just a little bit back from vertical, with the seat about the same height as the bars."

Like all other BMX riders, Dylan scans the British and American magazines for the latest racing and equipment news. Unlike most others, he can usually look forward to seeing his name there somewhere.

"That's one of the advantages about being with Ammaco, you get a lot of publicity. Once I started to see my name in the magazines it gave me more confidence, and I went faster. I know that the faster I go, the more publicity I'll get."

Maybe one day he'll be up to the level of his twin heroes, Britain's Tim March and USA's Eric Rupe (who coincidentally rides a Mongoose). If he doesn't make a long career as a BMX professional, then his ambition is to be a policeman. After all, he's already controlling the traffic almost every time he races.

Man behind the protective headgear is Dylan Clayton.

Heaven Help His Rivals

How 'big brother' came into BMX
– and what makes him go

Line up at the gate next to Garry Llewellyn and you get the impression that you're already riding for second place. He's the Marvin Hagler of BMX: outside competition he looks ferocious enough, but once on the race track he is even more fearsome than he looks. Every race is a demonstration of controlled fury. Heaven help anyone if he ever lets go.

When he started BMX racing in the middle of the 1983 season, his younger brother Wayne was already a number one plate-holder. It must have been tough for an older brother trying to take up a sport in such circumstances, but it didn't put Garry off. By the end of 1984 he had his own plate with number one on it, and looked like taking quite a few more.

"In the beginning it was the trophies that attracted me. Wayne kept on bringing them home and they looked good. I was two years older than him, and I thought that getting a few trophies of my own wouldn't be a bad idea, and that it would be easy. At first it certainly wasn't easy.

Garry, concentrating hard, can feel a challenge coming up on his right from the Raleigh rider, and is already moving to cut it off.

"Now the appeal of BMX is different. I like the competition. I love the racing because I win — and I like to win. When you're a member of the Ammaco team you're proud because everyone wants to know you, and lots of riders ask your advice."

At six feet four, Garry is the tallest of the team, more suited physically to basketball than BMX, you might think, and certainly he did dabble in this sport before he came to race on little bikes. Although a team member, he would be equally happy as a single sponsored rider, for he's basically a loner. While happy to help out Holly Jarvis with putting her bike together, he soon drifts off to watch the racing. He'll stand for moto after moto, watching the gate go down, concentrating on the starter's timing, working himself up towards the moment that he will be up there, launching himself forward at the split-second he reckons the gate will drop. Second-guessing the starter is one of the skills of top-class BMX.

When he left school he got a job with a local bike shop, Harry O's in West Wickham. His employers recognized the value of having a big-name BMX rider behind the counter, and were happy to give him time off to go on Ammaco

Garry Llewellyn raises a smile.

promotional assignments. Harry O's were also firmly behind the building of a BMX track in Beckenham, near Garry's home. Naturally Garry spends a lot of his training time there, practising starts and tactics with Wayne.

"In the beginning Wayne taught me a lot about how to ride. But then I started to watch other riders too, and learned from them, especially Pete Middleton."

You get the impression that when Garry meets Wayne in Superclass or Pro racing, there will be no quarter given — nor asked.

"Apart from training on my BMX bike, I do a bit of running and weight training. I've got a 10-speed for training too, but I don't really like to ride that unless the weather's warm."

Garry spends a lot of time on his bike. "You should ride it every day you can. I ride mine everywhere." He cleans it too. "My bike is very important to me. I keep it in top shape because that's what the fans expect of a top rider. They give you funny looks if you turn up to a meet on a muddy bike. After every meeting I check the bike over thoroughly, make sure that everything

is still tight and straight. Wheels are very important to me, the right balance between being light and strong. I'm going to have mine specially laced for racing, because Wayne already has his that way and they feel somehow stronger to me."

Because he is big and consequently heavy, Garry is hard on equipment. "I regularly grind up my bearings," he remarks. His size makes him look slightly strange on the 20-inch wheeled BMX bike, and far more natural on the 24-inch cruiser which he also races.

"Some big riders have longer frames, but I don't need one. I just use a laid-back seat post and a longer handlebar stem to give me the right position."

His size is an advantage in the rough-and-tumble which is Superclass racing. Although one step down from full professional status, Superclass riders can still walk off with up to £150 from a race meeting and still stay amateur, which isn't bad for a teenager.

"I practice gates a lot. Be fast out of gate and you have quite an advantage. But it doesn't end there. You have to know how to hold people off if they try to pass you. If they are going to try to elbow you, you have to be able to give them some back, otherwise you get knocked all over the place. If I feel a rider trying to lean on me I just tense everything, don't give an inch and concentrate on keeping pedalling. It's important to know how to keep the inside line on berms, and take jumps correctly."

Some riders are able to look back on a race and tell you every detail of their tactics and movements. Garry isn't one of them.

"When I'm on the gate I'm thinking real bad. But when it drops I forget everything and go. Sometimes when I've crossed the line I couldn't even tell you what happened in the race."

For a few years at least, Garry's future is firmly with BMX. "In the couple of years I've been racing I've seen a lot of changes. There are lots more riders and more tracks too. They say BMX bike sales have fallen, but that's because everyone has got their race bike for the time being. I reckon BMX is with us for a long time yet. And I hope that it's going to give me a living."

A steep jump approach has launched Garry into the air.

A number one plate brings its share of
admirers and regular autographs to sign.

Even in the great world of BMX, not all stories have a happy ending. Shortly before this book went to press, Garry Llewellyn left the Ammaco Mongoose team. It was a disciplinary decision by the manager Sue Jarvis, who had worked hard to get the best from the Llewellyn brothers and their undisputed talent, but felt that Garry should have a chance to re-start his racing career under other team colours. For a short while Wayne too thought he would be leaving Ammaco, but later reconsidered.

There are always autographs to sign. (*Evans*)

Spotted From A Park Bench

A total stranger's promise to Wayne Llewellyn came true

Imagine yourself mucking about in a park somewhere, just having fun going fast on an off-road fun bike called a Chopper. You've hardly heard of BMX, let alone raced. Then a complete stranger comes over and tells you that you could be European champion.

A dream? It was a dream that came true for Wayne Llewellyn, who went on from that strange introduction to win a whole string of number one plates, just as the stranger had promised.

"The guy was called Brian Smith. To me he had been just an old man sitting around on a park bench watching us. Then he came over and asked if I'd like to go to Buckmore Park and

race there. I didn't think a lot about it at the time, but then he called round to see my parents about it, and told them he'd make me number one in Europe. They agreed to let me join his team, and it progressed from there."

Wayne looks back gratefully on Brian Smith's contribution to his BMX career, which might never even have got started otherwise. Smith formed a team called Brian's Challengers, and in that first year (1982) Wayne took the number one plate in the 11-year-old age group.

"At the end of that season Brian agreed to let me go to Ammaco. I think he's in the Isle of Wight now, getting BMX going over there."

It was a move Wayne never regretted, and he

quickly felt at home in his new colours. "Being in the Ammaco team is like belonging to a big family. Everybody is friendly, and there are rarely any arguments. They treat me well, I like the bikes, and I like the manager."

The team became even more of a family for Wayne when older brother Garry was signed up. "When I was first riding for Brian I couldn't persuade him to go BMX-ing. Then finally I got him to have a go on the Wigan track and he fell off over the whoops. He didn't race for another year."

When Garry did start again, it was on Wayne's spare bike. This time he really did take to his younger brother's sport, and with spectacular results. Now everyone is waiting to see what happens when Wayne and Garry officially race against each other in the Superclass or Pro events.

"Normally we can't compete at the moment because of different age groupings. But in club and open meetings I've raced him two or three times and beaten him," says Wayne meaningfully.

Wayne has virtually grown up with BMX, after forsaking his other sports, long-distance running and basketball (he used to play for the crack Crystal Palace youth team).

"I first thought I might be good when I went to Buckmore Park and actually tried racing. I was fourth in my first event, and I won on my third time out. But things have changed a lot since then. Take the numbers for a start. It used to be 150-200 riders at a meeting, now it's over a thousand. In the 12, 13 and 14-year age groups it's much more competitive, with typically 90-odd riders at every meeting in each of those age groups. Now you've got to be really determined to win, and devote everything to the sport. In the beginning there were only two or three factory teams. Now there are loads of them. But it's a great atmosphere, and the racing itself is what really counts for me."

Wayne is a star, and likes it that way. You watch him at a meeting, and once he's put on his Ammaco gear he seems even taller than his six-foot-three. There are few things he enjoys as much as signing autographs and talking to the fans — and that's the way Ammaco like it,

Keeping the front wheel down on a speed jump.

because that keeps the team and the bikes in the public eye.

Part of his team involvement is turning out to promote Ammaco and Mongoose bikes at shops, exhibitions, on radio and TV, and here he is a natural. He has an easy smile which reveals his friendly character, and he'll happily talk BMX with everyone from his toughest rivals to the newest recruit in the under-7s.

The promotional work means taking days off school. "Auntie Sue came down to see the headmaster about it and fixed everything up. Whenever I have to miss any school, it means copying up the work which is done when I am away. When I leave school, I'd like to work for Ammaco doing racing and promotion full-time, like Andy Ruffell did."

The win that gave him the greatest buzz was his first European title in 1983. That year the

Practice makes perfect. Wayne tries a power wheelie on the lip of a berm.

championship was held over two separate "legs", the first on the impressive but dusty Wheels track in Birmingham, the second at Dijon, in France, on a track built as part of an indoor sports arena.

"At Birmingham I won every race until it came to the final, and I was leading that too until the last turn, when I went too wide and a boy came on the inside of me.

"At Dijon there was an open class too, and I was doing really well in that, until someone knocked me off. That put me in a really bad mood and made me really determined to win my age class, which I did by quite a long way. And because the boy who had won in Birmingham was only fourth at Dijon, I was the winner overall."

In 1983 he had his first crack at the world championships, at Slagharen in Holland, the first time the championships had ever been held outside the United States. But it wasn't his day. "In my motos I had the world champion and the runner-up. In all three rides I was

This is the way to take an obstacle. Wayne Llewellyn leads in this European championship 1984 shot, with both wheels firmly on the ground.

---

leading and then fell off, so of course I didn't get through."

Looking back to when he was new to the sport, what advice would he give to a beginner?

"Firstly, the bike. Don't get the cheapest you can. You need to spend at least £150, if you want to race. Then start to improve it gradually by getting better parts, until you can afford an even better bike. Then use your bike as much as you can. When it comes to racing, concentrate on getting a good start. If you get the holeshot, it means you can take your own line through the bends, and everyone behind has to react to what you do. That gives you more time to think about what you are going to do."

Above Sometimes you have to get airborne over steep jumps. Both leading riders are here trying to force their back wheels down for a stable landing.

Left Former Ammaco star Andy Ruffell, never seen without a crowd of admirers around him.

Right (top) The man who started it all, Ammaco boss Malcolm Jarvis.

Right (bottom) With so much going on at a BMX meeting, manager Sue Jarvis watches the racing while making sure daughter Holly has her helmet on properly.

Previous page
Good jump technique from Ammaco team rider Dave Morris, his front wheel hardly lifting over this speed jump.

In Superclass racing you rarely see a rider gain this much of a
lead. Garry Llewellyn leans forward over the bars to make for a
good landing on this speed jump.

Pete Middleton grabs air.

One of the team's most consistently successful
riders, Wayne Llewellyn.

Above   Recruited only partway through the 1985 season, West Country rider David Morris shows great style to hug the tight line around this strawbaled bend.

Left   You don't have to be around for years to get success in the pro ranks. Redline rider Geth Shooter moved straight into the money class without riding in Superclass, and found instant success.

Above   Two of Ammaco's three girl riders, Alexia Jarvis (nearest camera) and Keely Mulkerrins.

Left   Sometimes in BMX you have to take the hard way home. Garry Llewellyn limps back to the finish after a fall, but it didn't stop him helping the Ammaco team to first place in the 1985 Kellogg's series.

Sometimes waiting for your next moto can be a real yawn, Dave Morris finds.

Simply Speechless

Sometimes Ammaco have to move very quickly to sign the right kind of talent

For two years David Morris had a BMX bike and did nothing but ride around on it. As it happened, it was an Ammaco. Then one day he heard of a coach going from Bath, near his home in Trowbridge, to a big BMX meeting.

"I decided to go, and it was a good laugh, I really enjoyed it. I got a first, second and a fourth but didn't qualify for any finals. When I got home I told my parents how good the sport was, and how many people were involved, and they started taking me to more and more meetings. That's how it started."

Another two years of racing followed, and David gradually improved. Like many promising riders, he first found sponsorship from a local shop, in his case Plymouth's BMX Superstore. In 1984 he was ranked sixth in his age group (14) by NBMXA, one of the national governing bodies, and was also doing well in cruiser racing. This brought him better sponsorship from Curtis BMX, and the future suddenly looked rosy.

Then the Curtis team folded up, and David was unsponsored. It spurred him on even more, and he won the second 1985 national meeting of UKBMX, at Slough. The offers started coming — but not the one he really wanted.

On the Thursday after that win, the phone rang. It was Sue Jarvis, with an offer to join Ammaco Mongoose. She couldn't understand immediately why there was no answer from the Trowbridge end. David was literally speechless because his wildest dream had come true.

"I always wanted to ride for Ammaco and ride a Mongoose. They've been in BMX from the start, and they are the only team I really ever wanted to ride for. It's really worked out well for me."

David's chance came because of the sudden retirement of Steve Greaves, and that left Ammaco with a hole in the important 15 age group with the televised Kellogg's series looming up.

This is the kind of situation which needs quick action, otherwise important publicity opportunities would be missed.

"If you want to get into a sponsored team, make sure that the basics are right. Your bike has to be in good shape, and the position has to be right for you. Get plenty of practice on the bike, on the streets and on the tracks. Read all the BMX books and magazines you can, then go and watch the best riders to see how they do it.

"Whatever you do, don't be scared of other riders. In a tight situation tense yourself up and try to keep going whatever. If you find that the gap you're going for doesn't really exist, then ease up and watch for the next chance to go by, whether it's on a straight or on a bend. If things start to go wrong, don't panic, just think about what your're doing."

David Morris is a thinker, a planner, who looks like going far in BMX by using his head as well as his legs.

Keeping the energy levels topped up. (*Evans*)

Keys To Success

Advice from an American pro changed
Jon Greaves' outlook

Jon Greaves is the proof that it's easier to get to the top than to stay there. In a highly-competitive series of age groups he first took number one plate in 1982, dropped to second the following year, then became number one in 1984.

To be knocked off the top step of the ladder is often enough to finish a rider completely, but not so Jon. He just found a bit more determination and hit the top again at the next available opportunity.

He started racing in 1981, and did well enough at his one national event appearance to be ranked number 20. Ammaco picked him up for the 1982 season, and from then on he has never looked back.

There is no doubt that he has a lot of parental support. His Dad, Ken Greaves, encouraged him to train really hard for that 1982 season, and showed his own involvement by joining Ammaco as Northern Sales Manager.

"That training is probably why I got that first number one plate. But now I'm more experienced I don't train as hard. When I went to

Serious about his racing, Jon makes his way towards the starting paddock. (*Evans*)

Americans have been into BMX a lot longer, so they have the experience as well as the speed. So I spent a lot of my time watching them, to see what I might have been doing wrong."

From his American trip, Jon came back convinced that British BMX should use the transfer system of qualifying from motos. In this system, instead of each rider tackling three motos against the same opponents, with the qualifiers decided on points from the three rides, successful riders do not have to ride three times to qualify. The winner of the first ride automatically qualifies, and need not ride a second and third time. The winner of the second ride qualifies and sits out the third, in which the remaining riders battle for the remaining qualifying places. This system breeds riders who go out to win, rather than get good placings.

Experience is, Jon reckons, one of the keys to success. "That's why it is best if you start BMX very young, at seven or even less. You can get a lot of experience by the time you get into the higher age groups."

Equipment isn't all that important, he feels. "I am happy to use whatever the team is given. Of course good equipment can help, but you don't need all the best equipment to win. The only thing I am fussy about is my crank length. As I've got older I have gradually changed the length I ride. I use the winter to experiment with different lengths, and get it right before the season. I'm on 170 at the moment, which is shorter than a lot of others in my age group use, but it helps me to spin faster."

Jon loves all kinds of sports, and also plays a lot of football and squash. "I like fast sports. BMX gives me speed, and the thrill of winning."

What is it like when you are actually in the middle of a BMX race? "You don't have that much time to think, because you have to concentrate on keeping up with the other riders.

"The important thing is to watch for gaps opening up. When you see one, you have to go

---

America at the beginning of 1985 I met one of their pros, Ronnie Anderson, and he told me that I would be better just concentrating on riding my bike. Which is what I do now."

The American trip was quite an eye-opener. Mongoose of America helped a lot, supplying a team vehicle, helping with hotels, generally easing the Ammaco visitors into the US scene.

"We didn't race quite as much as we wanted, but that was probably a good thing. I came away with only one trophy for third place. But the

---

Jon Greaves (No. 2) has an elbow-to-elbow battle with a Frenchman during the 1984 Eurochamps.

for it, otherwise you'll end up staying behind, and the next thing you know it's the last straight and there's no more time to get past. Make sure the gap is wide enough to get through, go for the inside of him, and then try to take him up to the top of the berm."

Although he has a great sense of humour, Jon takes his responsibilities to the team very seriously. "We have promotions to go to, exhibitions and shop openings. Then we try to get our pictures into the BMX magazines, which is good publicity for Ammaco. And our behaviour has to be a good example to other riders."

Carrying such a responsibility can be a strain, however. Early in 1985 his brother Stephen, who had held a number one plate, retired from BMX. It meant Jon lost a constant companion and a regular training partner — they always used to go to the local track and practise chasing one another, which improved their speed.

"BMX has changed a lot, and one big change is the size of the meetings. They are really too large nowadays, so perhaps there is a case for qualifying for national events, to keep the numbers down. With so many long meetings, the season gets a bit wearying. In 1984 I was winning my races very well at the beginning of the season, but by the end I was only getting in the first three."

Jon is the kind of rider who is of immense value in a BMX team. He'll go far. "I want to be successful in BMX," he says. And it is easy to believe him.

Holly Jarvis in her race gear, ready for the call to the start. (*Evans*)

During a cold race meet, Alexia waits in the team van for her next race. (*Evans*)

The Jarvis Girls

A feminine slant on the appeal of life in a BMX team

Holly and Alexia Jarvis, the team manager's two daughters, have the time of their lives with BMX. Both race — and race well — but the enjoyment and the sheer fun of BMX weekends is more important to them than the actual competition.

Holly, the tiny of the team, is much more than their mascot, in 1984, a year off the top level in the 7-and-under age group, she was number three plate-holder, and number one in her region.

This is hardly surprising, considering her experience: "I first rode a two-wheeler when I was only two. I started in BMX when I was three, then retired when I was five. At six, I took it up again."

But she's far from being a BMX fanatic. "I suppose I started because of my dad. I like the racing, but the best part of it is making lots of friends. Speed on the straights is what I'm best at, and doing two-pedal starts. I like to practise a lot before races, but I don't really train. As I've moved up the age group the racing has got

Taking a wide line on this berm, Holly glances inside her before chopping down towards the point of the bend. (*Evans*)

easier for me, but a year ago it was tough because I was trying to beat girls who were older. Now I'm at the top of the age group."

Holly laughs a lot. Occasionally she sheds a tear after a bad race, which makes you wonder whether she might really be serious about BMX. And when you ask her about her favourite BMX rider she won't say — she just blushes when the name of Jon Greaves is mentioned.

BMX has taken her racing to several European countries. "I want to carry on riding for a long time yet," she says, but her eventual aim is to be a gymnast.

Alexia Jarvis had to be cajoled into BMX by her brothers. With Holly, Sam, Russell and Julian already heavily into the sport, she finally started to race in 1983, and had her first full season in 1984, gaining the number nine ranking.

"My brothers wouldn't stop nagging at me to try BMX," she recalls. "One of them even offered me five pounds and big bar of chocolate. Finally I had to start racing just to get a bit of peace and quiet."

She is still far from committed to the actual racing. "I like the racing but I'm not really serious about it. But then I don't think you should be serious about it unless you're a pro. BMX is a fun sport."

Her participation does have unexpected advantages, however. Like at school, where the last thing she gets is leg-pulls. "The boys actually suck up to me because I'm into BMX. They like it."

Her enjoyment comes from the travelling. "I enjoy the hotels the night before, all the messing about in different places, and the friends I make. We always stay up late, talking."

Despite her apparent concentration on the social side, she's a very competent rider. In 1983, her first racing year, she went to the European championships and fought her way through to the semi-finals.

"It was four to qualify, and I was in fourth place and just moving up to third when a girl fell off right in front of me. I finished fifth."

She thinks that many more girls should be trying BMX, and assures them that there is nothing to fear. "Just enjoy it, don't worry too much if at first you find it hard. With simply riding the bike you will get better. It's only in the top age groups where the girls are training really hard, and using weights like the boys."

Given the smaller numbers racing — perhaps seventy girls travel around the national circuit — they attract a high level of support and interest. And this is recognized by Sue Jarvis, who finds Holly and Alexia much in demand for promotions, videos and magazine articles where the aim is to interest the fair sex as well as the lads.

Alexia reckons she'll be racing hard "Until about 13, then I won't do as much. I don't think I'll end up with a job connected with the sport. I prefer to do something with animals, so maybe I'll be a vet."

What the Man looks like without his helmet.
(*Evans*)

Sam Jarvis shows a clean pair of wheels to his rivals.

The Lad They Call "The Man"

Sam Jarvis is not just the team manager's son – and has the plates to prove it

If you're the team manager's son at Ammaco, it means you have to try that much harder if you want to get on the team. Two of the Jarvis sons, although in Ammaco colours, don't get full-factory sponsorship because they don't race up to the standard of those who do.

Russell, the oldest of the children, has an on-off relationship with BMX which results in frequent retirements and comebacks. Julian, slightly younger, is a BMX fanatic and tries harder than most, but without the success he would like.

Only Sam, who has been in BMX for five years, and was in at the beginning with Ammaco, commands a place in the team by right. With two National number one plates to his name, plus a two and a three, his qualifications are obvious.

Because he has been around so long, and with such success, Sam is one of the most well-known BMX riders, and certainly the most well-known in his age group. That's one of the reasons he's called "Sam the Man".

"It's getting harder and harder now though," he says. "There seem to be more and more riders coming in at my age group. They called me Sam the Man almost from the start because I was winning a lot so I was the man everyone

Early days. Julian Jarvis brandishes a trophy.
(Ammaco)

Making sure his pedals are tight.
(Evans)

had to beat. But you have to remember at that time there weren't all that many riders."

He's an all-round sportsman, enjoying cricket, soccer, rugby and hockey at school. He has even done schoolboy moto-cross, but found that not quite as demanding as BMX because it doesn't need leg-power as well as tactics.

With BMX he's always looking for ways to go better. If he's at a track for the first time he will spend a lot of time practising, to find the right line on berms and over jumps.

Then he'll watch moto after moto, to see how other top riders are tackling the various track obstacles, and if it appeals, then that's the way he will do it.

One of the greatest experiences BMX has brought him was the team trip to the USA in early 1985.

"We were there for two weeks. We went to Disneyland and Universal Studios. And we raced against all the fast Americans. Racing against riders much better than yourself makes you push harder to get up to them, and that means you go faster when you come back to your own country."

The publicity value of being in a big team is something he values a lot, because with the publicity come the invitations to race all over Europe.

Ammaco's team also provide his BMX heroes. "I admire Wayne and Garry most, because they're big and muscly, and they always win. If you're big like them, rather than small like me, it's quite an advantage.''

So, small as he is, Sam has to rely on tactics rather than strength to carry him through. "If it's a good high gate I can get out of it fast. But I like berms on any track. During the race, if I'm not in the lead, I'm working out just where I can take the boy in front. I normally watch to see what line he's taking and then I try to go inside him. If I know I'm a lot faster, I just go on the outside of him. And if I'm in the lead, I concentrate on staying there, and if I think someone's coming up on me I sneak a look round and try to anticipate when and where they're going to try passing.''

Sam's advice for young newcomers: "You need a bit of courage to go out there and do it. Don't worry about falling off, and if you do fall off, pick yourself up and finish the race. Don't start crying if you get beaten — you have to learn not to be a bad loser.''

Eldest of the Jarvis brothers, Russell. (*Evans*)

Pardon My Elbows

Girls' racing isn't at all ladylike. Getting to the top needs toughness and a few tears

From Twickenham, the home of rugby football, comes one of Britain's top BMX girls, Keely Mulkerrins. She's not particularly big, nor is she tough to look at — in fact she's very easy to look at. But sheer determination took this West Londoner to the forefront of BMX in her very first season.

She started racing in 1984 "because my brother started, so I did." Her brother gave it a year, and then retired, but Keely went from strength to strength. After her performance in four National meetings, she was signed up by the Kuwahara team on a bike-only deal, with promises for better things to follow. With the 1985 season about to start, nothing solid had materialized from Kuwahara, so Keely went to Ammaco, and set about improving on her 1984 number three plate.

"BMX is a lot of fun, and its a challenge too. You get around a lot, make plenty of friends. Some people might think it's a strange sport for a girl to take up, but they usually change their mind when they come to meetings. There really are a lot of girls racing now. At school there's a lot of interest, and I'm always getting asked where I've finished at meetings. No one takes the mickey out of me, because they know I'm doing what I want to do."

Especially in the higher age groups, girls' BMX racing is no soft touch. "It can be tough at

Only the hair streaming out from behind the helmets tells you that this is a girls' race.
(*Evans*)

times, especially when there are eight of you on the gate, and some of the girls are big and strong. It's the same as in boys' racing, there are bound to be a few elbows sticking out.

"In girls' racing some of them haven't any style, but they can go really fast, so they get out in front and stay there. Others are good at tactics, but they haven't got the speed to get out front. I try to combine both.

"My tactics are to try to get a very good start. If I get in front, then I keep low on the berms, stay tight, and concentrate on pedalling all the way.

"If I'm behind at the start, then I wait until the leader goes wide on a berm and I cut inside them. They almost always go wide at some time, but if I think they're not going to, then I have to try taking them on the inside. What you should never do is follow right behind someone, because from that position it is almost impossible to make a good move to pass them."

Keely, who hides a shock of blonde hair underneath her helmet, is always out to improve, and to set herself new goals.

"The best thing that happened to me in my first year was to beat Sarah Jane Nichols. Everyone was saying that she was so good she couldn't be beaten, and I beat her fair and square. I knew I was going to do it sometime because I wanted it so much."

She pinpoints one of the advantages of the Ammaco team as the amount of help she gets from the other riders in improving her technique.

"Wayne did a lot to help me improve my gating technique, to really snap out of the gate. Before that I wasn't too good at starting, and I often had to make up a deficit over the rest of the track. The other riders watch, and if they see me do something wrong they will tell me how to do it better."

She had a taste of international racing early in 1985, when she won events in Lowestoft and Ipswich against Dutch and Belgian opposition, and is already looking forward to moving up the age groups towards a more profitable future.

"There is already talk of a Superclass for girls, and I don't see any reason why we shouldn't start to make a bit of money from BMX."

Keely Mulkerrins, the blonde bombshell.
(*Evans*)

It isn't all winning and making money though. Even top girls lose races, and Keely has come to terms with that.

"In my first year I used to get very annoyed when I was beaten, often just annoyed at myself for doing the wrong thing. There were a lot of tears, usually because of sheer frustration when I was going well and a girl knocked me off, or fell in front of me. But I'm over that now. If I get beaten, I just resolve to try harder the next time."

One of the sport's most consistent and respected riders, Pete Middleton.

From Team Ace To Ammaco Pro

Pete Middleton won Britain's first BMX event, and has been among the winners ever since

Top man in the Ammaco team, Pete Middleton is one of the elite band of riders who make their living out of BMX — the professionals. And he deserves to be, since he has a unique claim in British BMX, to be the first-ever winner. And it was on a Mongoose bike not too far different from the one he still rides.

It was in 1980. He and his mates around Walthamstow, a tough East London suburb, knew about BMX already, from watching an episode of CHiPS where the American motorcycle patrolmen got involved with a BMX bike chase.

"We were all freaked out by it, and were all trying to convert our bikes to look like real BMX bikes. We used to ride our bikes over forest land, locally, but of course there weren't any real races.

"Then one day a guy called Don Smith turned up and told us that there was going to be some demonstration racing in Brockwell Park, Brixton, with real BMX bikes, and he was looking for riders to take part. We were all very keen, so we had some races of our own, a little league, to decide who would go. The attraction was the chance to ride bikes built to BMX. When we got

there the track was downhill, using wooden ramps for jumps, with just one turn. I made the final and won. Danny Oakley, a Mongoose pro, was there, and I won a pair of Mongoose skinwall tyres."

Richard Barrington, who was marketing clothing for BMX, took Pete for his team, called Team Ace, along with Andy Ruffell, Cav Strutt and Nikki Matthews. But for a while Pete dropped out of the racing scene, until Don Smith came round to find out why, and to tell

Leaning over to keep a good line on a berm.

him about a new track at Buckmore Park, Chatham.

"I told Don that I couldn't race because I didn't have a bike, so he offered to lend me one. So I went there and won again."

Pete Middleton carried on winning races, and was well on his way to his first number one plate when sponsor Barrington had a dispute with UKBMX, and the whole team were banned.

"By the time the ban came off, I was so many points behind that there was no chance of getting the lead back."

In the meantime Don Smith had moved to become sales manager at Ammaco, and was looking to strengthen the team. He recruited Nikki Matthews and Pete, and the long tie-up between Middleton and Mongoose had begun.

But for a while Pete rode in the colours of Skyway, the American-made wheels which at the time were being imported and represented by Malcolm Jarvis of Ammaco. Only later did he officially ride for Ammaco.

"I suppose you could say that joining Ammaco created my whole BMX life. After all, to me Ammaco was THE name. It was like being a racing driver for Porsche or Ferrari. Their involvement in BMX, the amount of promotion work they have done for the sport, is unreal. I think if I had gone to ride for anyone else I wouldn't be where I am today."

For years Pete raced alongside Andy Ruffell. Now they are still friends, but in different teams.

Ammaco has certainly been a breeding-ground for stars. Imagine, at one time they had Pete riding alongside Andy Ruffell and Tim March. But did that create problems, with so much talent in one squad?

"At times, but not a lot of them. You have to remember that until we got to Superclass level, Andy and I were always one age-group apart, so we didn't race each other. I was in the same age group as Tim but we were good friends off the track. Once on the track it was fight all the way. Tim was with Mongoose before he became number one.

"While Andy was in the team, even though I was a year older, he was the one getting the limelight. This was because he has always been so forward and outspoken. He's very good at getting publicity.

"When Andy and I were actually racing together in the Superclass during 1984, he was beating me a lot. I suppose with us both in the same team we could both have lost if we started battling between ourselves. But anyway, partway through the season Sue, the manager, had a long talk with me about it. She thought I was faster than Andy and couldn't understand why I was getting beaten by him. I wasn't sure myself. A lot of times I could have passed him and I would have done if he'd been someone else. But after that talk my attitude changed dramatically. I started to treat him as just another rider, and then I started to beat him.

"But all in all 1984 was a bad year for me. Nothing seemed to come together. I was glad to get it over with. I always seemed to be crashing, often when I was in the lead, taking too tight a line. Maybe it was nerves or maybe I was just being silly and taking too many chances. Perhaps I simply wasn't as good, trackwise, as the others."

Andy Ruffell left Ammaco for the 1985 Raleigh squad, which left Pete as the unquestioned top rider of the team. He rode in the newly-formed pro class. And he quickly realized that it was more than just a change of name.

"First of all, pro racing is lot more competitive even than Superclass. In Superclass, you wouldn't get anyone fighting for places beyond about fourth or fifth. In among the pros, they are still battling for seventh and eighth places, because every place means more points and that means more money.

"Right at the beginning of the first pro season there were a lot of spectacular crashes, seven-rider stack-ups. I suppose everyone was nervous. But then everyone must have realized that it was better, whenever you went to the start-line, to stay upright. If you fall, you lose a lot of money. For that reason you don't see a lot of crashes in pro racing now. We take chances, of course, but not really risky ones.

"Because we all know each other we have a lot more respect, and we know what each of us can and can't do. Occasionally one rider does something bad to another one, but the bad feelings don't last.

"We are in a very special position because we have to work hard to promote the sport. Anyone who moans about us making money should remember that we are working to make the sport bigger and better. That's our responsibility, whereas you can't expect a 14- or 15-expert to do anything else but ride for fun.

"Our job is not just racing, but promotion too. For me every race day is a big promo, and I'm promoting myself much more as Pete Middleton than I used to. Before, I was just one of the Ammaco team, so I was signing autographs on team brochures. Now I'm still promoting Ammaco, but I'm signing on postcards and posters of myself. The sport needs to have professional personalities to look up to."

Pete points out that the pros actually do work harder. When they get to the main, they don't have one sudden-death ride like the other classes, but ride the main three times over, with points awarded each time.

"We came round to doing it this way to get a fair result, because most tracks were too short or too tame to give a good result over one ride."

Pete is already feeling the benefit of being a full-time rider. "Even though there wasn't a pro class officially until 1985, there were riders like Andy Ruffell, Trevor Robinson and quite a few others who were able to spend almost all their time training and racing. I was racing on natural ability and doing a normal job as a welder, so they ended up beating me."

Being a full-time professional has changed his daily routine, so that it all revolves around his obligations to Ammaco and to racing. From time to time, Ammaco need him for promotional work — shows, personal appearances, photo sessions — but otherwise he has to discipline himself to use his time well.

"I like to get a lot of sleep, but I also watch a lot of TV, so that means I don't get up early. Every day I am on the bike training, unless I have a promotion to go to. If I have to go down to the shops I often use my 10-speed. I eat anything my mum puts in front of me, but I like spicy food and curry. One night of the week I do weight training, mainly squats. Another night I play football. If I wasn't into BMX I would have

Life is tough in the pro class. Here Tim
March (2) tries to burst through between Pete
Middleton (6) and Mark White (11).

been a footballer, and in any case it takes a lot out of you, so keeps you fit.

"I like to train with Nikki Matthews. We get in a lot of riding together on local forest land. And in the evening we practise starts, sometimes up to a hundred each. He'll work the gate for ten starts for me, then I'll do it for him, and so on until we've done what we want. Starts are good not only for technique, but also for power. I keep my spinning technique good by using low gears when I ride around the streets, perhaps with a 39 or 40 ring, when I'd race on 42."

Although Pete is making a full-time living from the sport, the rewards aren't yet very high, but the purses are gradually climbing in value. In 1983 people were saying that a pro class couldn't work in British BMX, but both national bodies experimented with a Superclass. This went down so well that pro racing started in 1985. While the Superclass riders could win no more than £150 maximum, the pros had no set limit. A first at a Schweppes-sponsored national meeting would bring them £325.

"I suppose that this isn't much in itself, but that's only the start. There are other events with prize money, like the Kellogg's TV series. We get appearance money at some functions, and there are the retainers from our sponsors and co-sponsors. In the States they have been getting $5000 firsts regularly."

Three visits to the States have made a great impression on Pete, especially the team visit with Ammaco in February 1985 to Los Angeles.

"I learned most on that occasion. You can certainly see why the Americans are so good. They have no weather problems for a start, and can race all the year round. And they have the most fantastic practice grounds. The one we went to was totally rad, far more difficult than any track. Training there, being with them, you just have to improve.

"I stayed out there for a month, a fortnight longer than the rest of the team. I spent the second two weeks with Billy Griggs, a Mongoose pro, and went to meetings with him, and practised with guys like Greg Hill and Tommy Brackens."

Can you imagine one of Britain's best riders feeling like a novice? Pete realized he had a lot to learn — and quickly.

"What I noticed, just watching them, was that they pedalled almost all the time, much more than I would have done. And staying lower over jumps, which must make them better and faster. But as soon as I got the hang of it, I started to feel I was in their league.

"I went to an ABA National at Phoenix, Arizona, and in the first race I looked at my moto sheet and saw that I was racing Stu Thomsen and Brian Patterson, two former number one pros. But I was faster down the first straightaway and beat them into the first turn. After that, Bob Hadley, who is a team manager and has been in American BMX for years, told me that if I stayed there I could soon be making a lot of money."

Despite the threat of a foreigner taking bread out of their mouths, the Americans were very helpful.

"Also at Phoenix, Rob Fehd, the GT pro, told me that I was gating all wrong. The gate there was a fairly flat one, and I was still starting with my pedals in their usual position. He told me to have them down a touch because the start hill wasn't so steep. It made so much difference.

"That was typical of the welcome we got. People totally freaked out when they knew we were English. Everyone wanted to talk to us. They were all so very kind."

Even European-level racing takes some getting used to, Pete found.

"It is tougher than the average English rider expects. In the States the riding is relatively clean, because the tracks are so good it throws up the best riders, and everybody seems very experienced. In European international racing the others are just mad. The first time we went over there we were only just able to hold our own. The Dutch rode particularly hard. But now our riders are getting faster."

Europe was the scene of Pete's finest hour. He rates his best ride so far was getting to the final of the 14-plus open world championship at Slagharen in Holland in 1983.

"I was the only non-American in the line-up. But I was buzzing so much, so delighted to have reached the final, that I didn't get keyed up enough for the race itself. I could have kicked myself. Malcolm Jarvis has a picture of the start. All the Americans have got their back wheels clear of the gate and I've hardly moved. I was chasing for the rest of the race, and it was all over so quickly. I was sixth."

For Pete, getting keyed up is vital. And that doesn't necessarily mean going somewhere to be alone, and meditating.

"The pros are the first main, so I go up and watch all the semi-finals running off and try to key myself up. I think about winning. You have to concentrate, and I can do that whether the atmosphere at the gate is light or heavy, whether everyone's laughing or quiet. Once I'm keyed up for the first main, I stay that way through to the end. If I don't get keyed up, then I just blow the race. That's why I don't like signing autographs in the start area. If anyone asks, then I say I'll see them at the finish-line, which I do. Any other time I'm happy to talk and give autographs. I feel the older riders must look after the kids.

"Once the gate drops, then I go like hell. If I'm in front, then I concentrate on taking the best line through the berms, not making mistakes."

Experience tells most in BMX racing, Pete feels, but is happy to give this basic advice to all ambitious riders.

"On starts, the most important thing is to get a comfortable position. Tim March cocks his back wheel out a bit, and some others copy him, but it's just a matter of finding a comfortable position from which you can throw yourself forward when the gate goes down. If it's a traffic-light gate, I watch the lights of course, but on manual gates I look down at the track surface just beyond the gate. No reason, that's just where I like to look. Once the gate is down, I'm looking up at where I'm going. You don't have to turn your head to see where the others are. In the first straightaway you'll find that if any others are up with you or are ahead of you, you'll be able to see them out of the corner of your eye. If I can't see anyone, I go for the inside line on the first berm. The only time I look around is on the berms, to see if anyone is shaping to pass.

"On most berms the best bet is to take the inside line whatever. If you take a wide line it may be faster, but you're leaving room for someone to come inside you.

Recent trips to the USA gave Pete a new off-track style. Here he is sporting beard, glasses and pit cap.

"Try to stay down as much as you can on jumps, unless they're double whoops or a table-top. Don't go for maximum height because all the time you are off the ground you will be losing speed. For the same reason, on speed jumps keep pedalling as much as possible.

"In tight situations, stay strong on the bike. Hold on hard and try to keep your position. Keep your line rather than back-off. If people know you're going to do that they'll stay away from you.

"If you can see someone's getting into trouble, stay away from him. Keep your front wheel out of trouble because that's the one which is most vulnerable. If you realize you're going to fall, then get away from the bike. At the first signs I just bale out. Often you can run your way out of trouble."

Pete Middleton isn't one to back off in a tight situation, and has had his share of pizza elbows as a result. He reckons that this is part of being a top BMX rider.

"People like to talk about BMX as being a clean sport, but it isn't really. Healthy yes, but you can't expect eight riders to be racing for one spot without there being a lot of banging about. I'm as hard as any other rider, and they know I can handle it if the riding gets rough. There will always be a certain amount of bunching up in BMX, and I reckon I can come through it. To succeed in BMX you have to get out there and go for it."

The one thing Pete does insist on being clean is his bike. "For me it has to be in perfect condition. For some other top riders it doesn't seem to be important, because their bikes are just wrecks. I feel it can only help if you know nothing is likely to come loose in the middle of a race.

"I'm always checking my bike. If anything bends or creaks, I want to know why. If any component is suspect, I change it. Most of all, I check my chain, because the chain takes a lot of thrashing. Sometimes riders find that after each race their chain is loose, and they think their wheel has moved, when in fact it's the chain which has stretched, and needs changing. I also check the wheels a lot. If the spokes are loose, then you lose what is called rotational pull. You are just wasting energy. I taught myself to build wheels, so I build all my own. Tyres are very important, so as soon as the knobblies begin to wear, I change them.

"Apart from looking after your bike, the other important thing about BMX is enjoyment. Ride as much as you can, but don't get serious when you're young. You'll probably race better as a result. A lot of kids cry their eyes out when they come second. For me, if I finish in the top three, that's a good day's racing."

Pete has no doubt about his standing in the BMX scene, or its healthy future.

"I've been in BMX since the beginning, and I feel I'm as good as anyone in Britain. Sure, there have been times when I haven't been as dedicated, but then I've gone and pulled my finger out. People have always looked up to me, and I hope they always will.

"I see BMX going on for ever, and for the pros it can only get better. I shall keep racing as long as I can stay competitive, and have a chance of ranking in the top 10. If I retire, I hope to stay in the sport, maybe by opening a shop, or becoming a team manager. If the sport keeps on growing, then the teams are going to need professional team managers, and who better than an ex-rider?

"One recent happening shows me we're going places. It was during the Kellogg's series, and I went into the chemists to get some strapping for my arm. The girl in the shop asked me for my autograph. I wasn't in race gear, she had just recognized me. When that sort of thing happens, you feel you've done something."

Thoroughbred race bike, the Mongoose Californian. (*Ammaco*)

Getting The Bike Right

*Advice on making sure your machinery
is right for racing*

If you want to have the best chance of doing well in BMX racing, then you need the right kind of bike. Unfortunately among the big range of bikes which look as though they are made for BMX racing, there are some which will simply fall apart if they are regularly taken on to the track in competition.

To the experienced BMX rider such below-standard bikes are obvious. If you spend enough time on the tracks, you can almost see at a glance whether a bike is race-ready or not. So one way of finding out about bikes is to ask experienced riders. If you ask Ammaco Mongoose riders, they will tell you which Ammaco

or Mongoose bike is right for your age and experience, and which one you are likely to be able to afford. Remember that every full-factory rider has started out getting his or her own bike to begin with, so they know what your problem is. Every good factory rider, for the sake of the sponsor, should be able to tell you about the bikes whose name he carries. It's obvious he won't tell you the weak points of the bike he rides, but he will tell you the good points, and that helps.

You can be sure that any factory rider won't ride on a bike that continually lets him down, and bike-makers know that, so they work hard

Some of the accessories which make for a good transmission. (*Ammaco*)

to ensure that team bikes are just right. So if you take the catalogue and compare it with the bike that the factory rider uses on the track, then you can see where the bike has had to be "improved".

Don't do this blindly, of course. Every rider will have his own choice of pedals because some need very wide ones to cope with wide feet. Tall riders often use longer cranks, laid-back seat posts and handlebar stems which extend forward. All these personal changes are quite understandable.

You may not be able to afford a top race bike right from the start, but get the best you can, and then gradually improve it. BMX is a fashionable market as far as component manufacturers are concerned, so new models are always being launched. If you are tempted to buy a new item and you don't have a lot of money to spare, then ask yourself if it is really that much better than the one you have on your bike. Which is more important, for instance, changing your saddle because you like the new shape, or replacing a

tyre which is losing its tread?

When you buy your first bike to race on, pay attention to the frame first. It should be made of chrome-moly tubing — that's the actual tubing material, not just a chrome-plated finish (which is fine in itself). This kind of tubing is light and strong and ideal for racing. Frames can vary enormously in their handling — that's the way they feel when ridden. Some are easy to steer but feel sluggish, others are very lively, but difficult to steer over rough ground. Clearly something between these extremes is ideal. The best way to work out whether a frame design is going to suit is to try to borrow one for a short ride over some familiar ground.

If you want to do a lot of freestyle stunts on it as well as racing, then you may want to look at the various designs aimed at freestyle, possibly with twin or split top tubes, which allow you to stand with a foot either side of the saddle.

Pro-Class rims, drilled for lightness. (*Ammaco*)

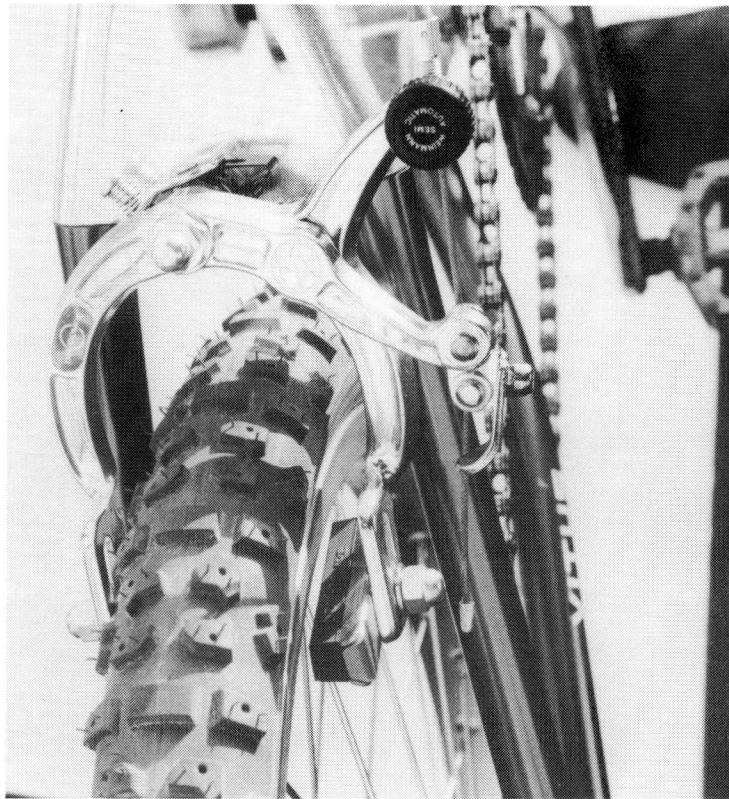

Sturdy caliper brake and heavily-studded tyre for tough conditions. (*Evans*)

Wheels are very important too, because they revolve, and any weight saved on revolving items, especially rims and tyres, is much more useful than the same amount saved on non-revolving items such as seats or handlebars.

Wheels are in two broad types, "mag" wheels or spoked wheels. Mag wheels have rims and big flat or girder-shaped spokes in one piece, made out of nylon or plastic. Mag wheels are great for freestyle and street riding because they are flexible. If you hit a big pothole, then they are likely to bend and spring back again, leaving you with little damage.

However, they aren't as good for racing as spoked wheels, with separate hub, spokes and rim. Spoked wheels are more rigid, so they don't soak up as much energy. If you ruin a rim (or want to change to a narrower or broader one) the wheel can easily be rebuilt by a good shop or specialist wheel-builder. If you bend the rim of a mag wheel, the whole wheel is for the junk-heap.

Go for alloy rims and hubs for lightness, and small-flange hubs because these will ensure a little more give in the spokes, to protect the rim over rough ground.

Rims and tyres can be of several widths, and you should choose these according to your own weight and size. A lot of under-10 riders

ride rims and tyres which are $1\frac{3}{8}$ or even $1\frac{1}{8}$ inches wide, but heavier riders will need $1\frac{1}{2}$ or $1\frac{3}{4}$-inch versions. For most top riders $1\frac{3}{4}$ is the choice, with the same width of tyre, but $1\frac{1}{2}$-inch rims are a useful choice because they can be used with either $1\frac{1}{2}$ or $1\frac{3}{4}$-inch tyres. However, you are unlikely to find $1\frac{1}{2}$-inch rims on anything but more expensive bikes.

There are two basic types of tyre tread, either a deep-cut knobbly tread which is ideal for tracks, or a smoother style which is right for street riding or stunts but does not offer enough grip for competition use.

You may wonder why coloured tyres have almost completely disappeared in top racing. This is simply because the black colouring element in the tread actually makes it harder and thus gives longer wear. So if you feel colourful, then be prepared to replace your tyres that much more often.

Pick a bike with a crankset that works for you. There are two things to consider here, the

Sporting mag wheels, the Mongoose Freestyle Ace. (Ammaco)

actual length of the cranks and the design of the chainring (also called a chainwheel or a front sprocket). Crank lengths can vary from 150mm to 185mm. In general, the shorter the cranks the easier it is to spin (pedal fast). If you prefer to push hard on a gear rather than spin it, then go for longer cranks, which give more leverage. Also, the shorter your legs, the shorter the cranks you should use. For the average under-

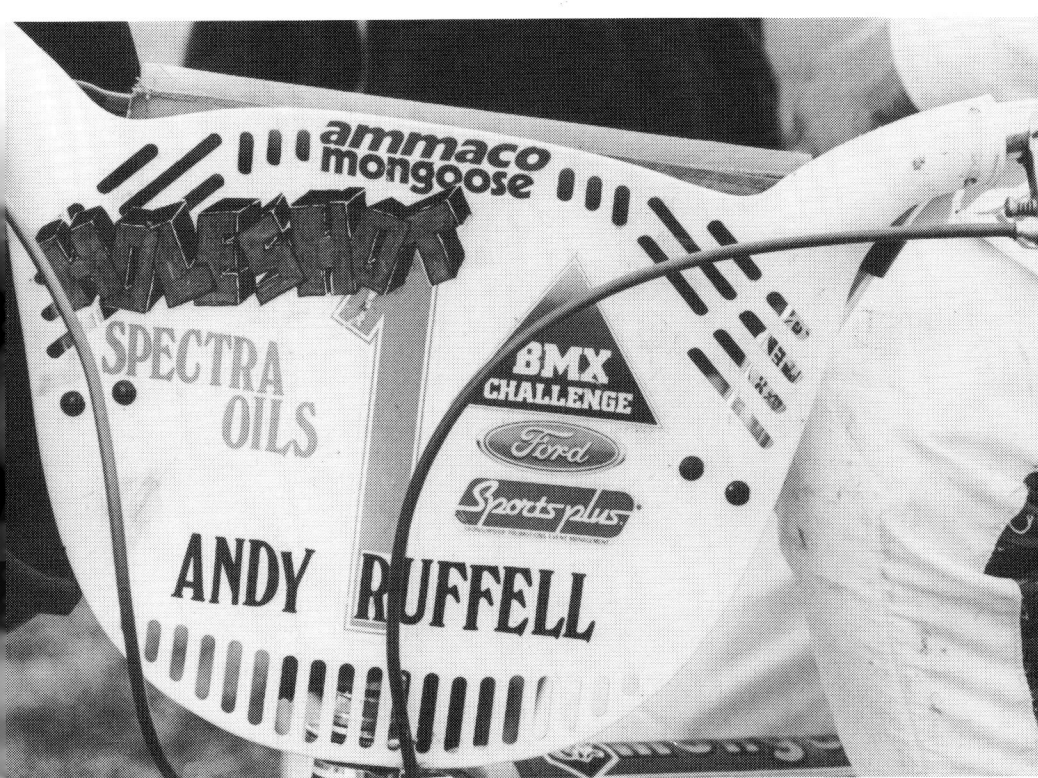

Race plates are a chance for personalization!

10, 170mm is plenty long enough, graduating later to 175 and only to 180 and 185 if you are tall and powerful.

Cranks come in two basic types. They are either one-piece, where the two crank arms and axle are one piece of metal, or three-piece, where you get two separate cranks and a separate axle. One-piece cranks are usually of chrome-moly (and should be for racing), while three-piece cranks are usually of aluminium alloy. There are chrome-moly three-piece sets but they are expensive, and favoured by many of the top riders. Whatever you get, make sure that the chainring can quickly be detached and replaced with one of a different size. To race well, you need to use the right gear for the track surface and length. The longer and easier the track, the bigger the gear. The shorter the straights, the more difficult the surface, the lower the gear. The best way of altering your gear after trying the track is to whip off the chainring and change it for a different one. For a suggestion, if you're an under-10 ride a 17-tooth rear sprocket, if you're older, then choose a 16-tooth. Then have in your race bag spare 42 and 44 chainrings, with 43 as your standard.

Incidentally, make sure your chain and rear sprocket match your chainring width, which will be $\frac{1}{8}$ or $\frac{3}{32}$-inch. If you have a choice, then go for $\frac{3}{32}$, which is lighter and smoother-running.

Pedals are a matter of personal preference or, to be more precise, the size of your feet. After all, the pedals have to take up your leg-power and pass it on via the cranks to the chain, and then through the freewheel to the rear wheel and finally to the track surface. If your feet are so wide and the pedals are so narrow that parts of your feet are able to sag over the outside of the pedal, then some of that leg-power is being lost. So if you have big feet, choose wide pedals (always remembering that wide pedals are more easy to "ground" when going round a tight berm while still pedalling).

There are two basic types of pedals, either the semi-platform type, where your feet press down on a block of metal, or the rat-trap type where the feet press down on the upper edges of thin plates of metal. The semi-platform offers more surface to press down on, but the thin edges of the rat-trap pedal plates will dig in better to the soles of your feet. So take your choice. Cycle dealers worthy of the name won't insist on you taking the pedals offered with a complete bike if they don't suit your taste, and will make a swap to another type if required. This in fact goes for many of the easily-detachable accessories, so if you don't like the odd component on a bike which you otherwise fancy, don't be shy about asking for certain parts to be changed, bearing in mind that there might be a small charge.

One of the other "points of contact" is the seat or saddle. Now in BMX you won't be spending a lot of time sitting down, except when you are pedalling around at ease. During racing the seat is only used as a stabilising point round corners. However, there can be occasions when you will be forced to sit down suddenly, your weight will come hard down on it, and it has to be made so that such contact won't be unpleasant.

First of all, make sure that the position of the saddle is right for you, so that when you sit down naturally you don't land partly over the back of the saddle (in which case push the saddle back or get a laid-back seat post) or on its peak (in which case slide the saddle forward). If there are any rough edges on the sitting area, then try to get rid of them or change the saddle. If it is a proper BMX saddle, then it will have a safety clip, which will stop the top of the seat post forcing up through the saddle top and causing you a nasty injury.

Third contact point is the handlebars, and here again the bike may need to be personalized. Not everybody with long legs automatically has broad shoulders. With handlebars, you have to consider two things. First of all, are the bars correctly set in the handlebar stem? You can rotate the bars forward and backward in the stem clamp to make the two places where you hold them either farther away or closer to you. You must experiment with this position so that it feels just right when you are starting fast. You should be able to get a good pull on your bars, trying to bring them into your chest as you thrust down on the pedals in those vital first few split seconds.

Protective pad sets can be decorative too.

Secondly, there is the actual shape of the handlebars. They can vary in raise (how high they are), width, and the angle of the grips. Here you have nothing to consider but your own comfort. Don't buy a shape of bars just because Pete or Garry or Wayne do well on them. They may not suit you. Generally speaking, the broader your chest and shoulders, the wider you'll need your bars. The longer your body, the greater the raise. Make sure that the angle of the bar ends doesn't make your wrist feel uncomfortable when you pull on them. The wrist should be straight and flat in relation to your forearm when you grip normally.

The best handlebars are made of chrome-moly steel. Although alloy handlebars are available and are much lighter, they are preferred only by lightweight riders.

Make sure of a good, sturdy four-bolt handlebar stem to hold your bars tight. If your bars will not stay tight in the stem, it could be that you have tightened the stem so much that the clamp has slightly squashed the bars, and they will have to be thrown away. Some stems extend further forward than others, and these are useful for taller riders to get an effective position.

Since BMX is about going fast rather than going slow, you may wonder if good brakes are really important. They are. You need brakes that will not only stop you once you've crossed the finish-line, but will also react instantly and positively during a race to any situation which needs a sudden slow-down. If you have to brake to get around a berm, then you should be braking late and hard, and that means having calipers you can rely on. The best ones can be adjusted accurately to alter the distance between brake-block and rim (to govern how quickly the braking comes into effect) but also to alter the distance of the brake lever from the handlebars, to suit the size of your hand.

If you study plenty of race photographs, you will see that some riders prefer to compete without a front brake. This saves weight and puts the braking only on the rear driving wheel. However, front brakes are far more powerful so can bring your speed down much more quickly if required, so if you tend to brake late, then go for a front brake too. The other consideration is the legal one. If you have no front brake, then you're breaking the law whenever you ride your bike on public roads, and that isn't likely to give the sport a good name.

Particularly for freestyle, rear coaster hub brakes are very popular. This type of brake works when you apply slight backward pressure on the pedals. It has to be built into the rear wheel, since it is part of the hub mechanism, and is clamped to the left-hand chain stay for anchorage. Freestyle frames have a specially brazed-on bracket to accept such a brake. Although such a brake can be used in racing, it is unnecessary because of the weight.

When you are getting your first racing bike, the first consideration is a chrome-moly frame, then look for light wheels and quality brakes. Anything else is not so important, and can be gradually changed as you can afford it.

If you are unsure of whether the bike you think is a BMX racer will actually do the job, then ask the shop owner to give you a guarantee. I hope in any case that you will be buying through a regular cycle dealer and preferably a BMX specialist, in which case you will get the best advice.

One good guide is to buy a brand which, like Ammaco and Mongoose, runs a factory team. Such companies not only have top-line race bikes, but also run "econoqual" models, quality-economy versions which are right for racing but don't cost as much as the full team bikes.

One final word: don't forget your safety pads. For racing you must have padding on crossbar, over the head of the stem, and on the cross-piece of the handlebars. All the governing bodies insist on this to avoid injury in crashes which throw the rider forward. Although pads can be highly decorative, they are there for a purpose, and the rider who only fits them for racing and doesn't use them for all his riding is just being stupid.

Pete Middleton shows how eye-catching race gear can be.

Into Top Gear

Racing clothing isn't just for show

One of the elements which makes BMX so eye-catching is the brightly-coloured gear that everyone rides in. BMX race gear has its own changing fashions, in designs and materials, but it always has to do its job of protecting the rider.

It is no coincidence that the designs and materials used are very close to those used in powered moto-cross, which has an even greater need for protection.

Although first aid is available at every event, and there are always a few cuts and bruises to treat, it is not unusual for a crash victim to pick himself or herself up, have a quick brush-off, and walk away, completely unhurt.

This is because a lot of the crash contact with the ground is sliding contact, which with the right protective gear need not cause any injury. More of a danger is unwanted contact with bikes, and this is why the regulations forbid any bits which stick out unnecessarily, like reflectors, chainguards, and lamp brackets. Part of the function of handlebar grips is to pad the ends of the handlebars to minimize risk of injury.

But your first line of defence is the race clothing, from top to toe. Of course you can ride in a long-sleeved unpadded tee-shirt if you like, you can get away with jeans and ordinary trainers. But they won't do the best job, and you shouldn't be satisfied until you have kitted yourself out in proper race gear.

The rules call for every rider to wear a protective helmet, long sleeves and trousers, and gloves, and your gear should be checked when you have your bike scrutineered. But you owe it to yourself to do more than the minimum to stay within the rules.

Probably the most important item is the crash helmet. These are very similar to motorcycle helmets in design and construction, only with slightly lighter materials being used because the speeds involved in BMX aren't as high. As yet there is no British Standard for BMX helmets, so the only real guide as to whether the helmet is really effective is to see whether top BMX riders wear one. However, if the helmet is from a well-known manufacturer, you have little need to worry.

Even the best helmet won't do its job if it doesn't fit you. It should be snug on the head, even before the strap is secured, and be absolutely immovable once strapped on, no matter what head-shaking antics you get up to.

There are two basic types of helmet design, full-face or open-face. Full-face helmets are similar to those worn by fighter pilots. They

Good head protection is all-important. Here is an open-face helmet combined with face-guard and goggles.

extend right around the front of the mouth, nose and chin, so that only the upper cheek-bones and the eyes can be seen through the porthole in front. The drawback with full-face helmets is that the front part obstructs your vision of riders coming at you from the side, so you don't see them until later.

For this reason open-face helmets are most popular. These cover only the skull and the ears, with additional protection for the face coming from mouthguards and chinguards which press-stud on to the side of the helmet and which fit so close to the face that vision is not impaired. Helmets also have pop-on visors, useful in bright sunlight, and also as a first line of defence for the face if you fall.

Some riders like to use goggles, but these can also pose problems. In muddy weather they can get splashed, and suddenly you can't see properly. And even in decent weather the rims

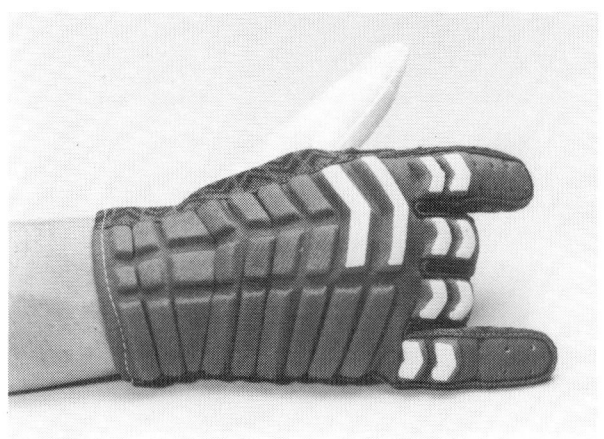

Protective race gloves.

of the goggles can obstruct your vision at the edges. Better to restrict your use of goggles to windy days and dusty tracks.

Race tops come in cotton, perforated nylon, polyester or similar lightweight material. Their main feature, apart from their colourful look, is the protective padding which is found at the elbows and sometimes also over the shoulders. The top need not be skin tight, and should be worn over another vest, so that if you fall the top layer slides against the bottom layer and cuts down the risk of grazes.

Race pants need to be really tough, and for this reason are usually in closely-woven nylon. They carry padding up the front of the shins, over the knees and sometimes over the hips. Remember that hips, knees and ankle bones are likely to get cut up in an unprotected fall, and that during the racing you can sometimes make contact with a whirling pedal. The fit needs to be good and close, with nothing flapping at the ankle which might catch in the chain. However, you do need room over the knee for it to bend during pedalling without any great restriction. The best race pants are cut to take account of this.

Shoes are a cross between old-fashioned plimsolls and trainers. Specially-made BMX shoes are widely available, and the American ones favoured by most of the top riders are simply cut with no gimmicks — just the occasional chequer to give an individual look. The secret is in the sole, which should be thin enough to "feel" the pedals without being so thin that the soles of your feet hurt every time you press down.

Other BMX shoes are more elaborate, either cut higher over the ankle, or with more supporting panels on the outside of the foot. If you fancy more protection than the straightforward simple BMX shoes, then you can buy separate ankle protectors. Most riders don't bother. Some don't even wear socks because they feel they get a better grip of their shoes that way. Simplicity is probably best, because with simple shoes your feet and ankles can move much more easily, and you are less likely to have any restriction or chafing because you have been pedalling fast.

Finally, gloves have to be a good close fit, otherwise you risk losing your grip on the bars and the race. What type you choose is a personal preference, and some riders change according to the temperature. You need protection on your hands because the palm is particularly painful if you crash on it — and you usually do, if you have time to throw out your arms to break your fall.

The broad choice is between cotton gloves and leather gloves. Cotton or woollen gloves are light to wear and can give a close fit. Usually the palms are studded with plastic or rubber to improve the grip. But they are little protection compared with leather gloves, which should be of thin, supple leather with protective patches over the knuckles and the backs of the fingers. The best leather gloves are cut shorter on the insides of the hands, because they are designed to be used with the hands gripping.

If you want more protection than standard race gear, you can buy strap-on elbow and arm pads (sliders) and gaiters for lower leg protection. But with proper BMX clothing these extra aids shouldn't be necessary.

One of the national bodies, UKBMX, is recognized internationally, and brought the European championships to Birmingham.

BMX Today And Tomorrow

The sport has made a big impact on the public but it still needs to grow

In her other "job" as national secretary of UKBMX and one of its international delegates, Sue Jarvis wants BMX in Britain to grow even bigger than it is now. She wants every BMX-er to realize that they are part of a movement which covers the country and reaches out to other parts of the world. Which is why, when she is driving the Ammaco team van and sees a kid with a BMX in the street, she gives a peep on the horn in recognition.

And recognition is what she wants for BMX in general. Because although it is one of the country's most popular sports for children, not all local authorities welcome it, or give active assistance.

"If the sport is to get much bigger, it needs to be taken into the schools as part of the school curriculum, like football or cricket, tennis or athletics. It is happening in certain schools. My kids go to a school where they have a BMX track. A lot of public sports centres now have BMX tracks, and because a lot of schools have their sports periods at these centres, it would be easy to take in BMX as part of the general activities."

At least one national association has realized that for thousands of children, there is no bike but a BMX bike. RoSPA, the Royal Society for the Prevention of Accidents, has devised a version of its cycling proficiency test which is specially applied to BMX riders. It tests the riders' skill over rough ground as well as in normal road traffic situations. It makes learning safe riding quite a lot of fun.

She thinks BMX riders can do a lot to help themselves locally. Through parents, they can press local councils for some kind of facilities to use their BMX bikes in safety, away from public roads.

"Ask your local authority for a track, or failing that for land which can be used for off-road riding, which can be used for a track if you can get it built yourselves."

Wherever there are no facilities, BMX riders risk getting themselves criticized and losing goodwill because, let's face it, BMX bikes have to be used somehow, and that could mean doing some impromptu stunt riding in cul-de-sacs, bumping up and down kerbs, making footpaths and pavements dangerous for pedestrians by riding on them.

Just because you think you can control yourself on your bike, it doesn't mean you won't upset or frighten other people — especially old people — by riding it where and how you shouldn't.

So it is important to make the point to anyone

in authority that BMX is good, healthy sport and deserves the right kind of local backing so that the sport can be practised in the proper places.

Parents are very useful for this kind of help, for taking you to races, and for generally getting involved. But there are limits. Sue Jarvis, as a race official, has seen just how some parents take things too far.

"I would like to see some parents be better sportsmen, and set a better example to their children. Too many of them can't bear to see their children lose, so they end up pushing them to complain, when the child wouldn't normally want to. They get really upset at the other children and at the officials, when it isn't really their affair.

"If the kid loses, I don't mind if he cusses a bit and gets upset. It is understandable, and it only lasts a moment. BMX is short and sharp, the excitements and the disappointments are that

The sport has a big following from all age-groups. (Evans)

way too. Parents should try to help their children take the knocks and the pain. It's part of life."

BMX is a family sport, if you just let your parents involve themselves the right way. Meetings up and down the country turn out to be not just a series of races, but also a social function for all the families involved. All the Ammaco team rate the friendships they have made through the sport as one of its great benefits, and few sports let parents become so closely involved as BMX does. As supporters, chauffeurs, trainers, mechanics, marshals and organizers, mum and dad can have a great time too.

BMX could be even bigger if the Government gave money in the form of grant aid, through the Sports Council. Unfortunately that can't happen while the sport has more than one governing body. Because of arguments about how the sport was run, officials within UKBMX argued and the rival body, NBMXA, was formed. Both bodies run their own programmes, but now their rules are different only in small details. Riders tend to compete under both associations. If the two bodies can get together and get the sport under one ruling organization again, the way would be clear for grant aid from national and regional sports councils.

As it is, most of the factory teams like Ammaco ride the UKBMX meetings as a priority, because UKBMX is recognized by the international governing body (IBMXF) and that means acceptance for European and World championships.

Some of the Ammaco riders came up through the NBMXA ranks, and did well there, getting a lower UKBMX ranking than they deserved because they didn't concentrate on the meetings of one or other body.

Because of there being two organizations, it is difficult to work out how many racing BMX riders there are. UKBMX has about 4,000 licence-holders, NBMXA a similar number, but many riders hold licences for both. On top of this, there are lots of riders who compete only at club level, and never take out a licence. The net result is about 12,000 actual competitors covering the country.

Sue Jarvis knows that there are potentially many more riders. Some can only compete at club level because they haven't got the transport help from parents to go to meetings farther away. Others actually go to race meetings and never race. Are you one of those?

You have to be a little bit brave to ride your first race, but you can make it easier by going along to your local BMX track on practice night, where you can get used to riding fast around the track with riders around you, but without actually having the stress of a race.

In the next chapter, you can learn how to get started.

These top riders are in classic race gear, but jeans and shirt will do to start with — just make sure you have a good helmet and gloves.

Getting Started

For the newcomer to racing

Every member of the Ammaco team was once on the outside of BMX racing, not knowing quite what it was all about, but curious, and eager to get racing.

It isn't difficult to start, if you know how. And knowing how begins with knowing where. The key to starting BMX racing is to find your local track.

That shouldn't be too difficult. Look in your local BMX shop for details of local meetings, then go to one. Ask the kids there about the local club, and you're halfway to racing.

In fact, if the race meeting is a local one, you can probably start racing then and there, provided that you fulfil a few basic conditions. These concern your bike and your clothing.

It has to be a BMX-style bike, with wheels no larger than 20 inches (unless it is a 24-inch cruiser, for which there are special events). Anything which sticks out unnecessarily must be removed for safety. This includes lamp brackets, handlebar mirrors, bolt-on reflectors (wheel and pedal reflectors are OK), luggage carriers and removable chain guards. You need only have one brake, and this should act on the back wheel, but of course two brakes are quite allowable. You must have protective padding on the crossbar, the handlebar cross-strut, and over the head of the handlebar extension. The ends of the handlebars must be covered with grips.

All the nuts and bolts must be tight. Although this will be checked by the scrutineer before you are allowed on the track, it is best to do your own checking and tightening beforehand, to save time and embarrassment.

You will also need a race number plate so that the judges can identify you. Any number will do, but the lower numbers identify the rankings obtained by the better riders the previous season, so stick to a three-figure or four-figure number to avoid confusion.

If you haven't a number plate, there are a number of clever ways of creating them from things like paper picnic plates. The organizers will usually help out.

You must have good protective clothing. A BMX-style crash helmet is essential, complete with mouthguard, and you must wear long trousers, a long-sleeved top, gloves and shoes. You can improvise with jeans, a jersey, ordinary gloves and trainers, but you will clearly need a special helmet.

Organized meetings at official tracks have

The way to the top. Riders climbing the start-hill towards their appointment with Mr. Starter. *(Evans)*

insurance, which you pay for either through your licence fee (more about licences later) or by buying a "day insurance" to cover you for the meeting only. It isn't expensive. This gives you insurance cover for personal injury, or against claims from other people involved.

If you think you will want to race outside normal club meetings, then you will need to apply for a licence from either UKBMX or NBMXA, the two national governing bodies. Which you choose depends on the tracks you choose to race at, and whose regional and national competitions you prefer. There is little to choose between them, except that UKBMX has international recognition. There is nothing

to stop you getting a licence from both organizations if you want to race under both codes. Many do.

Apart from automatic insurance cover, the licence officially registers you with the national body you choose, and at regional or national meetings you can score points towards your regional or national ranking at the end of the season, which in turn gives you your ranking for the following year.

Rankings are in individual age groups, decided by your age on January 1 of the year concerned. Normally age groups cover only one year, except for the under-7s, who race together, and the girls, who have age groups covering two years.

At every meeting the basic procedure is the same. First you get your bike and race gear scrutineered, then you go to register, producing your licence if needed at this point. National meetings and some other events attract so many sign-ups that registration is necessary by person or by post no later than the day before.

Race officials sort all the entries into age groups and then into motos — the name that BMX riders use for qualifying heats. When this long task is completed, the moto sheets are posted up, so you can see who you will be racing against. Each moto has a number, which indicates the order in which the motos are run off, usually starting with the youngest riders and the girls, and moving up through the age scale, so that the Superclass and Pro riders provide the final racing of each moto series.

When all the motos have been run off once, and every rider given points according to finish position, the entire moto series is run off a second and finally a third time. The points for each rider in your moto are totalled, with the best four going through to the next round, perhaps a semi-final, but sometimes a quarter-final or even straight to a "main" (final) if there aren't many riders in the age group.

If there are only enough riders to make up one moto, then the points classification over the three runnings of that moto decide the final order. This is called the Grand Prix system.

Once you get beyond the moto stage, further qualifying is simple, with quarter- and semi-finals being run only once, and the top four of each eight in a quarter-final going through to two semi-finals, for instance. The main is run only once, except in the case of the pros, where it is run three times.

In every race you will have to know your position on the starting gate. This will be posted along with the moto sheets, and changes for each moto. For rides after the motos, you draw for starting positions.

If you take the advice from Pete, Garry and Wayne, the top Ammaco riders, you will have watched some motos before yours is called to the starting paddock, where riders assemble in their starting lanes and move up the start hill towards the gate as the motos in front of them are sent off. Watching the other motos start helps you to get used to the starter's own individual starting rhythm, and decide how long he normally pauses after shouting "Riders ready ... pedals ready ..." before shouting "GO" and letting the gate drop in front of you. As the gate drops, you should already be lunging forward. From then on, after keeping in lanes for the first 15 metres, you can follow whatever line you choose, although you should avoid deliberate body contact.

Take the Ammaco riders' advice during the racing, and listen to the finish judges as you cross the line and are told your position. Go to the finish paddock just beyond the finish line, to a point marked for your finishing position. Pause while your number is taken by the recorders, and then go back to your car or team area and relax until it's time to get ready for your next race.

That's what to expect from your first race. If you get eliminated in the motos, don't pack up and go home disappointed. Spend more time watching how the successful riders do it, watching their technique and the lines they follow over the various obstacles. Look at the bikes and accessories, talk to other riders — ask all the questions you can think of, and then use the answers to be in better shape for the next meeting.

The Last Words

In this book you have learned a lot about the Ammaco team and, I hope, a little about the fun sport of Bicycle Moto-Cross.

Through the story of the team, the riders who make it up and the other people who pay for it and run it, you can see what a lot of effort goes into making sure that Ammaco is represented on the start-line at all the major meetings — and among the winners too.

Reading this book, you will probably have wished that you could ride for Ammaco or one of the other factory teams, and enjoy the glamour of being one of the country's best riders. One day it could happen to you.

Even though the top riders get enormous attention from the fans and the media, you have to remember that they all started out, like you, as youngsters with an interest in BMX. A year before this book was written, some of the riders had only just started racing, and Ammaco didn't even know about them, let alone want them on the team. This is how quickly events can happen in BMX. So if you think that being in a big team is out of the question for you, then you are quite possibly selling yourself short.

For BMX is about basic things that all youngsters can do naturally, and all enjoy. About going fast on bikes, being daredevil over rough ground. About taking a bit of machinery apart and putting it together again better than it was

when it started. About trying to be better than the next kid — and trying again if you fail once.

Through getting to know the Ammaco crew you will hopefully have realized what is really important about succeeding in BMX racing. Getting the bike right for you, learning the moves, and developing the courage to "go for it" when the opportunity arises.

But remember too the other message which comes across so strongly from these top riders. That winning isn't everything, and certainly is nothing without enjoyment.

*For more information on your nearest BMX club, write to these two national organizations:

UKBMX
5 Church Hill
Staplehurst
Tonbridge
Kent TN12 OA7

NBMXA
Litho House
Heath Rd
Ashton-in-Makerfield
Wigan
WN4 9DY